A LOGISTICS IT STRATEGY FIRM PERFORMANCE & GENERATION Y CORPORATE SOCIAL RESPONSIBILITY

A LOGISTICS IT STRATEGY FIRM PERFORMANCE & GENERATION Y CORPORATE SOCIAL RESPONSIBILITY

Archanaa Arumugam Kappan
Logistics Executive
Pure Circle Sdn Bhd

Tracy Hiew Yeap Teng
Senior Sales Executive
Behn Meyer Malaysia Sdn Bhd

Inda Sukati, PhD
Assistant Professor
CCBA, Dhofar University, Sultanate of Oman

Abu Bakar Abdul Hamid, PhD
Professor of Marketing and Supply Chain Management
PUTRA Business School
UPM Malaysia

PARTRIDGE

Copyright © 2020 by ARUMUGAM, TENG, HAMID, SUKATI.

ISBN:	Softcover	978-1-5437-5889-4
	eBook	978-1-5437-5890-0

All rights reserved. No part of this book may be used or reproduced by any means, graphic, electronic, or mechanical, including photocopying, recording, taping or by any information storage retrieval system without the written permission of the author except in the case of brief quotations embodied in critical articles and reviews.

Because of the dynamic nature of the Internet, any web addresses or links contained in this book may have changed since publication and may no longer be valid. The views expressed in this work are solely those of the author and do not necessarily reflect the views of the publisher, and the publisher hereby disclaims any responsibility for them.

Print information available on the last page.

To order additional copies of this book, contact
Toll Free +65 3165 7531 (Singapore)
Toll Free +60 3 3099 4412 (Malaysia)
orders.singapore@partridgepublishing.com

www.partridgepublishing.com/singapore

Contents

Chapter 1   Strategic Logistics Challenges 1
Chapter 2   Documentary Analysis 12
Chapter 3   Exploration Procedure 30
Chapter 4   Discovery Facts 47
Chapter 5   Dialogue and Decision 63
Conclusion 79
References 81
Appendix 1 95
Appendix 2 103

Chapter 1   Foreword 113
Chapter 2   Desk Reviews 122
Chapter 3   Procedures 141
Chapter 4   Discovery 156
Chapter 5   Deliberation 178
Conclusion 191
References 193
Appendix 213

LOGISTICS STRATEGY, ORGANIZATIONAL STRUCTURE AND LOGISTICS INFORMATION TECHNOLOGY IN MANUFACTURING FIRM PERFORMANCE

CHAPTER ONE

Strategic Logistics Challenges

Background

Malaysia is one of the most diversified economies in the world with the services, manufacturing, agriculture and mining sectors providing the right balance to economy of the country. Being the world's 24th largest trading nation, Malaysia's manufacturing sector plays an integral role in enabling the growth of the country's supply chain system. The development and continuing evolution of the logistics role are obvious in the last two decades in Malaysian manufacturing sector (Shaharudin, Rashid, Wangbenmad, Hotrawaisaya, & Wararatcha, 2018). Rather than being viewed as a supportive industry to other functional areas previously, now, it has been regarded as a strategic industry on its own. In fact, logistics had already become prominent and acknowledged as a critical factor of competitive advantage in other advanced countries like the United States and United Kingdom.

The increasing importance of the logistics industry has been resulted from the expansion of the international trade as well as the globalisation strategy of companies in their business. The dramatic expansion in the external trade in ASEAN countries such as Singapore, Thailand, Malaysia and Indonesia recently, has resulted an increase in demand for more efficient and effective logistics services (Rehman, 2017). In the past, companies are not aware of the advantage of having an effective distribution system and thus have not given sufficient priority to the development of effective distribution strategies and structures. However, the transformation of economy from agriculture-based to a trade-driven based as well as the development of international trade within the last decade has stimulated awareness that logistics system plays a critical role in facilitating the country's economy (Kaur, 2004).

Logistics system is the most commonly discussed topic among practitioners and academia. Logistics management involves some parts of supply chain management that plans, implements, and controls the efficient, effective forward and reverses flow and storage of goods, services and related information from the point of origin and the point of consumption in order to meet customer's requirements. The Malaysian logistics industry has been recognized globally. In fact, the global Logistics Performance Index (LPI) in 2018, by the World Bank has ranked Malaysia at the 41th place out of 160 countries all over the world (*https://lpi.worldbank.org/international/global/2018*).

In 2003, MIDA introduced specialised facilities such as the Integrated Logistics Services (ILS) and International Integrated Logistics Services (IILS) to encourage the growth of Malaysian manufacturing companies and logistics industry performances. As at April 2018, MIDA has approved 89 ILS projects with total investment of RM5.9 billion. Among the states in Malaysia, Negeri Sembilan registered with a total of 151 approved logistics investments that mainly related to the chemical, transportation equipment, engineering, electrical and electronic, and food and beverages sectors. The prime responsibility of logistics systems in organization is to implement multiple strategies to handle the requirements and expectations in order to optimise inventory cost and to improve the firm's profitability ratio (Green, Whitten, & Inman, 2008).

Despite of the remarkable expansion of the industry, particularly in Malaysia, there has been very little published research and studies in the area of logistics and supply chain resulting in a very limited dissemination of information for the purpose of coordination, learning, advancement and etc. In the Malaysian context, very few studies are focusing on logistics system's contribution towards the organization performance especially in manufacturing firms. Consequently, as a part of a large-scale research project on logistics and supply chain management, this study begins by examining the factors that affect the organization performance of manufacturing firms in Negeri Sembilan, from a logistics perspective.

The prime objective of this study is to expand on the established paradigm by testing and evaluate the relationships within the context of logistics strategy, organizational structure and logistics information technology on performance of manufacturing firms in Negeri Sembilan, Malaysia. Management literature has established paradigm as a means to assess direction of the relationships and the interactions, influence and along with its effects in between independent and dependent variables.

In this study, firstly discussed the effect on the relationship between key firm's components of logistics strategy, organizational structure, logistics information technology (LIT) and organization performance of manufacturing company which directly related with the logistics setting were carry out. Then, questionnaire survey conducted in Negeri Sembilan and results were analysed. Based on the findings, few suggestions recommended to implement effective logistics strategies, organizational structures and the logistics information technologies to improve financial and non-financial performances of manufacturing firms. In addition, policy makers, manufacturing management representatives and government sectors are encouraged to develop more effective policies and practices for managing the manufacturing firm's performances.

Problem Statement

In past studies, Ittner, Larcker and Randall (2003), Schellenberg (2013) and Gokus (2008) has identified that consistent evidence of firm's utilization of a broad set of organization performance via logistics strategies and there are congruence effects among strategy, structure and managerial performance criteria on performance of the company. However, study conducted by Bawayarapu (2005) examine the effects of various types of strategies in logistics on the firm's performance revealed there is not a clear relationship between the strategies with financial and non-financial performance of company and need further examination especially in manufacturing sector.

Sosiawani, Ramli, Mustafa and Yusoff (2015), Knott (1998), Adewale, Adesola and Oyewale (2013), and Rehman (2017) has identified that strategic planning able to helps organization to achieve great performance level and there is positive relationship among variables. Smith and Reece (1998) and Wu (2018) examined the concept of adaptation strategy methods and they found a moderating effect of organizational culture on the relationship between strategic change and firm's performance. Aloulou (2018) analysed and examined the significance between strategic orientations as well as the role play by them and the effect on performance of manufacturing firm. The authors found there is a significant relationship with variables and the findings are mixed, unclear and therefore there is a need to investigate further the relationship between strategy and performance.

Similarly, Handfield and Bechtel (2001), Borella, Barcellos, Sachdev, Russ and Galelli (2017), and Agbaeze and Obi-Anike (2017) studied and examined the effect of organizational structure on the performance of selected manufacturing companies and they found that structure is significantly affects organization's financial performances. In another perspective, Bohte and Meier (2001), and Nchorbuno, Shafiwu and Ayamga (2017) investigate how the organizational structures shape organizational performance and they identified that there are limited effects on performance when organizations addresses the intermediate level structures.

Apart from that, Smith (2007) and Troyer (1995) investigate structure of firm and the impact of the operating performance system and the results shows that its incongruity and can negatively affect the system's performance evaluations. On the other hand, Tavitiyaman, Zhang and Qu (2012), Banerjee and Srivastava (2017), and Espino-Rodríguez and Gil-Padilla (2015) found that organizational structure to have a medium effect on the correlation between both of these strategies and performance of an organization. Based on the above discussion, the findings are mostly significant but still there is gap between the variables and therefore there is a need to investigate and examine further the relationship between structure and performance of the manufacturing firms that based in Negeri Sembilan, Malaysia.

In the past studies, Henry (2016), Kimani (2015) and Wilson, Iravo, Tirimba and Ombui (2015) found there is a direct correlation between Information Technology (IT) and firm's performance and addresses the inconsistencies and gaps in theoretical frameworks of IT and performance of firm. Ayantoyinbo (2015), and Ratna and Kaur (2016) examine the effects of IT on the performance of distribution channels from logistics systems stand point and they found there is moderate effect on their firms performance due to IT systems. Roberts (2015), Cortes, Serna and Gomez (2013), and Zakaria, Zailani and Fernando (2010) conducted a study to examine the effects of logistics on organization performance with information technology as mediator and the results showed IT has no influence on the logistics service quality.

Based on the discussion, understand that logistics system plays an important role in determining the performance of an organization. However, the findings are mixed and contradictory and therefore there is a need to study and investigate further the relationship between organizational structures, logistics strategy and logistics information technology. This paper has provided an overview of perceptions and feedback of management representatives of manufacturing firms in Negeri Sembilan on the logistics factors that affect the performance of an organization.

Research Questions

The study is mainly designed to answer the following question:

1. Does the logistics strategy significantly influence the organization performance of manufacturing firm?
2. Does the organizational structure significantly influence the organization performance of manufacturing firm?
3. Does the logistics information technology significantly influence the organization performance of manufacturing firm?

The answers and justifications to the research questions will gain from findings retrieved from response of managers, management representatives, logistics industry experts and other professionals in the manufacturing organization that operates in Negeri Sembilan.

Research Objectives

This study evaluates the knowledge-based theories with statistical analysis to determine the impact of independent and dependent variables. The objectives of studies are:

1. To investigate the relationship between logistics strategy and the organization performance of manufacturing firm?
2. To investigate the relationship between organizational structure and the organization performance of manufacturing firm?

3. To investigate the relationship between logistics information technology and the organization performance of manufacturing firm?

Scope of Study

This study is to examine and survey the logistics middle and top-level management representative's perceptions regarding logistics strategy, organization structure, logistics information technology and organization performance in manufacturing companies. The survey administered with a random sampling method among management representatives (managers and top management) from various manufacturing firms who were selected from list of companies that registered under Federation of Malaysia Manufacturers (FMM), Negeri Sembilan. The objective of this approach is to examined and investigate the various strategies and structure terminologies that exist with logistics information technology processes in manufacturing firms in Negeri Sembilan, Malaysia. The respondents draw from representatives or industry specialist from logistics-based manufacturing firms by using random sampling with a questionnaire for a required survey of 132 samples (as a minimum requirement).

Significance of Study

The management of logistics under the supply chains system has become more demanding due to high competition in market (Green, Whitten, & Inman, 2008). Thus, management of manufacturer's sector are seeking for alternative methods which helps to manage the logistics system effectively. In addressing the severity of this problem, Yavuz and Deligonul (2017) recommend few actions and strategies that focus on the logistics systems in order to reduce operational and overhead expenses. It's inclusive of "sharing relevant information's among the distribution channel members, maintaining proper communication within suppliers, involving specialists and experts as and when required and establishing effective performance" which measures as part of the continuous improvements (Yavuz & Deligonul, 2017).

This study is structured to assess relationships between key components of the firm and targeted financial and non-financial goals outcomes. The study directly examines the influence of company representative and manager's perception (middle and top-level management) of logistics on relevant variables. Furthermore, the logistics research setting provides insights from this vital part of the manufacturing firm, which is often not addressed in strategy related research or study in Malaysia.

Contrarily, the revolution of information technology in industries especially in manufacturing sector permits an integration in logistics systems and improved information sharing with communication abilities by improving the performance of an organization. Furthermore, Arthur, Stephen, Wilson and Ronald (2016) found that the extensive use of communication technology by the vendors who being as logistics service providers will helps to transforms the information flow with multiple levels of the logistics systems. Apparently, communication technology highly contributed to the development of logistics services with supply chain management (Tang, Wong, & Foon, 2018).

Apart from that, this study has design methodology which generate a visionary to research questions and hypotheses to determine the relationship of dependent and independent variables of logistics; logistics strategy, organizational structure, logistics information technology (LIT) and organization performance improvement. The correlations and the effects of the independent variables and the strength of relationships among variables were examined through multiple regression coefficients and has identified that the four variables are very important elements for manufacturers who are exploiting to manage the logistics system and company performance successfully.

Operational Definition

This section provides the definition of terms which are frequently used throughout this study in order to avoid misconception, misunderstanding and misinterpretation of the meaning of the terms.

Logistics Strategy

Logistics strategy define as an action that managers take to attain one or more of the organization's goals (Baiyi & Fan, 2011). In this study, logistics strategy refers to activities that results in supply chain performance (in manufacturing and distribution), value added system, information's that flows among channel members, competitive customer service and collaboration with dealers or distributors.

Organizational Structure

Organizational structure is a hierarchical arrangement of rights and duties of an organization, lines of authority and communications process (Banerjee & Srivastava, 2017). In this study, organizational structure refers to less traditional structures with ability to change business environments, effective leadership, time management and critical thinking, organizational realignment by closing the structural gaps and power distance.

Logistics Information Technology (LIT)

Shaharuin, Rashid, Wangbenmad, Hotrawaisaya and Wararatcha (2018) elaborated logistics information technology is a platform for managing a business data effectively and integration of IT systems to improve organizational flexibility and readiness to respond to changing environment at minimized costs in logistics settings. In this study, LIT is more specified as integrating new technology, integrated inventory system, transportation and warehousing planning system, creating strategic opportunities by real-time tracking and accurate delivery systems.

Organization Performance

In business perspective, organization performance is a matter of making sure that the functional requirements are being met (Tang, Wong, & Foon, 2018). In the context of this study, organization performance is ability to meet promised delivery dates and customer requests, perform value added services in distribution processes, achieving high volume output and meet customer expectations and company goals (financial and non-financial).

CHAPTER TWO

Documentary Analysis

Introduction

The chapter two reviews the relevant literature regarding the development of the logistics strategies, organizational structure, logistics information technology (LIT) and organization performance in conceptual framework. The sequence for this chapter is follows as review of prior studies by review journals, research associates with performance of manufacturing organization with related variables and examination of studies that investigate the challenges faced by the logistics systems of supply chain management. The sources of literature review including review of articles, articles, past and current research or studies on related subjects and business periodical journals. The review inclusive of current methods of mitigating the problems and the continuing implications of the trends in the logistics system due to better strategy and technological robust in logistics information processes of manufacturing firms in Malaysia.

Overview of Organization Performance

Tang, Wong and Foon (2018) define performance as a key financial and non-financial metrics that used to measure health of the organization. Rehman (2017) identified and define organization performance by measurement classification in terms of annual rate of growth in net sales, number of customer complaints, customer or employee satisfactions towards organization, annual rate of growth in earnings per common share and after-tax return on equity. However, most of the Malaysian companies conceptualized organization performance as measurement and benchmark of key elements such as productivity, sustainability in market, profit, cost effectiveness and/or cost reduction of the organization.

Ability to meet customer expectations especially on quoted or anticipated quality and delivery dates on a consistent basis is consider as one of the organization performance measurement. Then, on time delivery (OTD) is one of the metrics to measure the efficiency of supply chain processes in an organization. It is being as an indicator of how capable is the organization to meet customer demand in terms of the requested delivery date (RDD). Apart from that, historically customers have expected basics criteria's like quality service and fair pricing, but modern customers have much higher expectations such as proactive service, personalized interactions and connected experiences across distribution channels.

In today's business world, as integration with Information Technology (IT), disruptive companies leverage breakthroughs in online clouds, mobile apps, social media's and artificial intelligence technology to deliver personalized, valuable and immediate experiences, so that the customers have more choices than ever. As a result, they grow to expect this superior experience from any business they engaged with and perceived firm's performance matches with customer expectations and company goals.

Besides that, Henry (2016) reveals that researchers often use organization performance and its antecedents in their studies with varying interpretations of what constitutes with "performance of the company". Organization performance considerations have ranged from customer or employee satisfaction to cost effectiveness. However, performance also interpreted as measurement of the specific goals or achievement, the level of target achieves and being as plot of future strategies of an organization (Green, Dwayne, Inman, & Anthony, 2008).

The actual performance figures will provide the researchers with more opportunities to evaluate the effect and significance of performance in a manufacturing organization. Ideally, actual numbers are desired by most of the management or organizations but perceptual performance measurements still are useful to the researchers. Even if the study is across many industries by perceptual, performance measures and provide the researchers an option to assess the effect of the research model on performance as an interest to management representatives and head of departments in an organization (Bhandari, 2014).

Similarly, perform value added services for customers during the warehouse or distribution processes is essential as a part of the organization performance. To meet the increasing demands for product customization and delivery compliance, the organization should able to provide value-added services to help the customers to reduce their inventory footprint of finished goods. Expeditors' value-added services are ranged from simple to complex which enable variety of logistics delivery models that improve customer service while mitigating inventory and transportation costs.

Most of the Multinationals organization grapple with their own unique problems and each must come up with its own innovations. Still, while the focus varies from company to company, many manufacturers have tried similar approaches. With a tightly coordinated network of plants in high cost end markets and low-cost manufacturing centres, Multinationals can achieve new economies of scale and cut costs by eliminating redundant processes. Experts says, they must focus on specific changes and at individual sites by articulating a vision shared by the entire organization in order to attain the lowest total supply chain cost by achieving high volume output (economy of scale).

Performance of an organization can be split into two categories; namely financial and non-financial performances and this is essential for sustainability of a business, to increase the value of the company and the satisfaction of stakeholders. The financial performance and achievement are the one that most people think of for companies and they involve profits, costs, turn over revenue, marketing costs and so on which reflect the performance in terms of financial growth and financial efficiency. The rest else falls into the category of non-financial performance. Non-financial performance is mostly relate to the current customers, potential customers or customer services whereby to expand sales to existing customers, to increase customer loyalty to the weaker brands (current customers), to develop new products for current and potential customers, to improve customer satisfaction with customer services.

Further, other non-financial performances might relate to other areas, such as technology. For example, when a manufacturer increases efficiencies with security and virtual technology for their distributors and retailers or the organization's people; for example, when a software developer aligns performance and reward management with corporate core values. On the other hand, performance may include different aspects such as order fulfilment rate, safety stock, obsolete product as well as the number of warranty claim (Shaharudin, Rashid, Wangbenmad, Hotrawaisaya, & Wararatcha, 2018).

During the year 2000, organization performance measure has become the multi-million industry for most of the firms in Malaysia and the firms ask for calculate the business performance in their business. They were using many new methods to calculate, just like activity-based costing, accounting and shareholder analysis. Some of them are using the new measurement framework, mostly by having the balance scorecard and business excellence model to measure the organization performance. This method is to calculate the internal performance and external benchmark with the external parties (Aloulou, 2018).

Based on literature search, there are many factros that affecting the overall performance of a firm. However, Tang, Wong amd Foon (2018) has discussed that how the logistics system could help directly on the organization performance and many researches has highlighted logistics factors have significant impact toward the organization performance. In order to improve the performance, the manufacturing firms in Negeri Sembilan should implement the logistics improvement tools such as strategies, structure and information technology to reduce the cost and focus on few areas like storing, distribution, customer cost efficiency and quality services (Zakaria, Zailani, & Fernando, 2010). The business also will gain the competitive advantage by having the effective logistics system.

Overview of Logistics Systems in Manufacturing Firms

Logistics is core function of supply chain along with marketing, operations, finance, procurement, new product by research and development (R&D), customer service and determinant that measures variables of performance that affect an organization (Arthur, Stephen, Wilson, & Ronald, 2016). Logistics seen hike up in interest in either theoretically or practically and it has not been matched with other related development in research methodologies (Angappa, Nachiappan & Thanos, 2015). Logistics also described as process of managing the products, finance, information between business functions (Yavuz & Deligonul, 2017). In another perspective, logistics management define as part of supply chain management (SCM) that "plans, implements and controls the efficiency, effective-forward and reverse-flow, and storage of goods, services and related information" between the point of origin and the point of consumption in order to meet customer's requirements (Kachitvichyanukul, Sethanan, & Dawson, 2015).

The tremendous technological change and the accelerating globalization of business have forced companies to look beyond cost and to emphasis speed, quality, agility and flexibility of their manufacturing facilities. Competitive advantage for many manufacturing companies now lies in their ability to effectively implement on-going product and process innovation, superior manufacturing, continuous improvement of quality and reliability (Q & R) of existing products and developing a continuous stream of new quality products (Yusuf, Gunasekaran, Adeleye, & Sivayoganathan, 2004).

Manufacturing sector play an important role in the economy of Malaysia and it is the single largest contributor to the economy (56.5%) and directly employs more than 9.3 million of the total employment in the country and contributes 72.3% to the total exports *(New Economic Model - Eleventh Malaysian Plan:2016-2020, MIDA 2019)*. Despite its spectacular achievements in the manufacturing sector, Malaysian manufacturers face several challenges from the logistics context. The main challenges are to improve competitiveness, quality and on time delivery (OTD) to global markets, while competing against imports from cheaper sources in the domestic market.

Malaysia has performed well on some of these measures of competitiveness, but there is certainly a lot more room for improvement. The 1990s and millennium have seen the quality revolution spreading beyond manufacturing and industrial revolution 4.0; many organizations are forced to change their old strategies and management styles, and to develop better strategies to allocate available resources in order to remain competitive. Identifying manufacturers' competitive priorities and manufacturing practices are considered a key element of manufacturing strategy in this research. In this view, the study been conducted to identify the effect of logistics factors towards manufacturing firm's performances in Negeri Sembilan, Malaysia.

Theory of Resources-Based-View (RBV)

Theory of Resource Based View (RBV) has been widely used by the researchers in business and management context. RBV is primary use to identify the competitive advantage of the firm by combined both valuable, tangible and intangible resources (Kraaijenbrink, Spender, & Groen, 2010). Based on previous researches, some has used RBV theory as the based framework for research and mainly focus to identified the factors that affecting the organization performance in manufacturing sectors to find out the factors that affecting the performance of the firm (Tan, Ng, Fong, Chong, & Sukumaran, 2016). The resources or factors should be valuable, rare and non-inimitable by others (Barney, 2001). Other researchers said prefer as long as the resources can bring the strong performance as it can be defined as resources of the firm (Morrison, Manion, & Cohen, 2011).

Besides that, there were some of the studies use RBV theories to test the competitive advantage of the manufacturing firms by adapting logistics systems and the three major determinants in their study; the strategies, structures and information technology (Husso & Nybakk, 2010) The logistics strategies, organizational structure and logistics information technology (LIT) are expected to guide the formation of the performance of the manufacturing firm.

The conceptual framework for the study is shown in Figure 2.1. A total of three independent variables are used to analyse the relationship with organization performance of manufacturing firms.

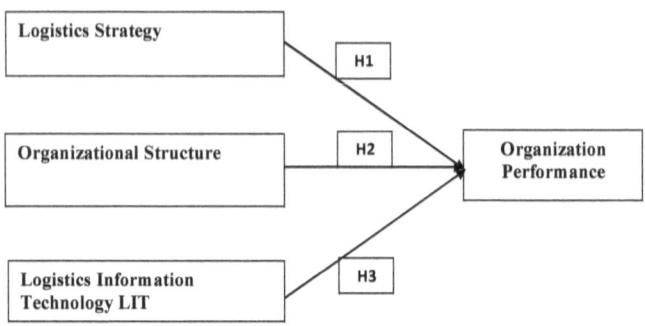

Figure 2.1: The conceptual framework based on RBV theory

Hypothesis Development

Logistics Strategy

Logistics strategy define as a result of the goals of the firm and the demands of the environment in which the firm competes with or in (Green, Whitten, & Inman, 2008). According to Kyengo (2014), logistics strategies focus on "how both internal and external business processes can be integrated and coordinated throughout the logistics processes to better serve ultimate customers and consumers while enhancing the performance of the organization". Furthermore, strategy development experts recognize the importance of matching a firm's abilities with the demands of the marketplace (Ittner, Larcker, & Randall, 2003). Logistics strategy is mirroring the missions of an organization and the prime goals which must be achieved with efficient ways in handling the limited available resources in the specific organization.

Today, more organizations are realizing the importance of strategic logistics system, both from a cost base management standpoint and the way to improve customer responsiveness which examine the concept of logistics strategy in their evaluation of leading-edge firms (Wu, 2018). Logistics strategy deals with company's objectives which related to the firm's inter-relationships with others, inclusive of customer's contacts along with channel members and service providers (Kyengo, 2014).

Ittner, Larcker and Randall (2003) identify that organizations make more extensive use of a performance terminology via financial and non-financial measurements rather than firm's logistics strategies. However, they find medium correlation for the hypothesis that more or less extensive measurement than predicted by the firm's logistics strategy that adversely affect the performance of the organization. Apart from that, Gokus (2008) found that the level and type of logistics strategy that used in an organization does not directly reflect the relationship between organization's performance and market orientation but indirectly does affect the performance of an organization. It has found that, environmental factor moderates the relationship between type of strategy used in logistics and the business performance probability in an organization.

Specific definitions for type of logistics strategy are provides in Table 2.1. Aloulou (2018) found that most of the manufacturing firms respond with a process strategy compare to the other two variables (market and logistics or distribution channel). Specifically, 58% selected processes, 28% selected market, 9% selected the channel and the remaining 9% opting for "others". More recently, this construct has generated similar results in research conduct by Hosseini, Tekmedash, Karami and Jabarzadeh (2019). The process strategy garner

50.0%, market 25.5% and channel 15.4%, with 9.1% selecting for "others".

Table 2.1: Specific type of logistics strategies

Process	A process-base strategy is emphasis on achieving efficiency from managing manufacturing, scheduling orders, purchasing materials and physical distribution as an integrated system with logistics processes.
Market	A market-base strategy is concern with managing a limited group of logistics activities for a multi-division business unit or across multiple business units. The logistics organization seeks to make joint-product-shipments to different product target groups and seeks to facilitate the customers.
Channel	A channel-base strategy is concern about managing the logistics activities, perform joint-ventures with dealers and distributors. The strategic orientation plays an important role on external control management. Significant volume of finished goods is typically maintained either as forward or downstream in the distribution channel.

In different circumstance, Sosiawani, Ramli, Mustafa and Yusoff (2015) focus on study and determine the factors that might contribute to the performance of an organization. Strategic decision is believed to be able to drive organization to achieve extensive performance. The results of the study show a positive relationship between strategic planning (strategies in terms of logistics service) with performance of the organization. The study carry-out by Rehman (2017) found that applies the concept of multiple strategic orientations for the purpose of improving business to business (B2B) performance is positively correlated. The results support the presence of strategic and active orientation between logistics and organizational orientations for the purpose of improving the performance level in terms of service quality and financial performance.

Similarly, Kyengo (2014) conducted a study to examine the relationship between manufacturing strategy and operational performance among firms in the metals and allied sector. The findings show that manufacturing strategy formulation following a formal process with both top down and bottom up participation thus ensuring that the capabilities and competencies of the organization along with inputs (Kyengo, 2014). Many authors reported that successful past performance tends to lead to resistance in strategic changes. However, few researchers highlighted that greater strategic change in poorer performing firms than in better performing firms. The above discussion shows that findings appear and most of the results reveal there is positive relationship between logistics strategies and performance of an organization, however needs further studies and researches in related aspects. Therefore, based on these arguments, the following hypothesis is posited:

H1: *Logistics strategy has significant relationship with organization performance in manufacturing firm.*

Organizational Structure

Organizational structure defines as key element of the firm's abilities to respond to the changing in market-place or even in a specific industry. Nchorbuno, Shafiwu and Ayamga (2017) define organizational structure as formal allocation of duties, responsibilities, roles and the administrative protocols to control and integrate work related with activities including those cross formal organizational boundaries. Specifically, organizational structure in logistics settings is comprise of formal lines of authority, communication, information and data that flow along those lines. To capture a more complete understanding of organizational structure, it is subdivided into three specific dimensions that consists of centralization, formalization and specialization (Toriello, 2017). Variations of these three dimensions have been used in the past and will be explain further in the next sections.

Banerjee and Srivastava (2017) define firms with a low degree of centralization and formalization as flexible and organic firms with high degree as mechanistic firms, use it as a way to indicate the continuum of the structure of the organization. These three aspects will address in detailed in the following sections and will be cover briefly to demonstrate the development of related hypotheses.

Centralization

The centralization or decentralization of decision-making authority is one method of defining structure in organizations (Banerjee & Srivastava, 2017). A centralised management approach indicates that one or a limited number of top managers retain most of the decision-making authority in an organization. While, a decentralised management concept indicates that more levels of the organization layers have the ability to make decisions (Espino-Rodríguez & Gil-Padilla, 2015).

Formalization

Formalization reduces an organization's need for employees to seek out new information within the firm to make decisions (Schellenberg, 2013). Unfortunately, this strict environment of rules and regulations may also reduce the firm's ability to respond to innovative ideas due to the bureaucracy involved in making changes in organizational structure (Banerjee & Srivastava, 2017).

Specialization

Specialization addresses how activities and tasks are allocated across employees or positions within an organization (Borella, Barcellos, Sachdev, Russ, & Galelli, 2017). As employees begin into specialization, they become more knowledgeable about related procedures and how new ideas can be used. Furthermore, productivity will improve when employees are able to target one responsibility or task (Banerjee & Srivastava, 2017).

While, Schellenberg (2013), has conclude that organizations selecting prospector strategy, managerial performance criteria and structures should congruent to have higher performance than the organization whose structures and logistis systems werein congruent. Managerial performance criteria is use in evaluating logistics managers and a significant results found that's organizational or logistics structure in a manufacturing company will effect the performance positively (Schellenberg, 2013).

Similarly, Borella, Barcellos, Sachdev, Russ and Galelli (2017) study the aspects that related with service capability and organizational structure which contribute to the performance of logistics service providers in the B2B context. The survey consists of multiple scales to represent the construct variables related to schedule deliveries, transportation, warehousing, port operations, customs clearance, organizational structure, service capability, inventory control and business performance. They identify that the ability to meet technical and operational for a better business performance, especially in-service contract with customers (Borella, Barcellos, Sachdev, Russ, & Galelli, 2017).

Apart from that, Nwonu, Agbaeze and Obi-Anike (2017) study and examine the effect of organizational structure on the performance of selected manufacturing companies in Enugu State, Nigeria with a focus on pharmaceutical manufacturing firms. The study found that structure significantly affects organizational performance except in its growth objective. Banerjee and Srivastava (2017) analyse and examine organizational structure in Indian context and the effects on the business performance which measure by financial and service performance. The results show that organization structure is positively significant with hypothesis and an organization is group of people who are trying to achieve a common goal.

After examining the literature, it can be concluded that the relationship between organizational structure and performance of an organization is not clear and needs further study and examination. Therefore, based on the above arguments, this study seeks to propose the following hypothesis:

H2: *Organizational structure has significant relationship with organization performance in manufacturing firm.*

Logistics Information Technology (LIT)

Logistics Information Technology (LIT) define as knowledge and abilities that address the logistics responsibilities within the organization. Understanding the information processing is important to ascertain appropriate research questions which related to information technology (Bhandari, 2014). Organizational information processing theory addresses how the structure of the organization facilitates information exchange, specifically in firm's information processing requirements (Olah, Karmazin, Peto, & Popp, 2017). Logistics information technology or LIT is the process of creation, utilization, support, study, design and management of computer-based information-systems, software and hardware applications which related with supply chain system, specifically in logistics (Tang, Wong, & Foon, 2018).

LIT is not limited solely to computers thoughts, but it also widely related with the process, management, structural and dealing of an organization with sub-cons, vendors, suppliers, third party warehouse and customers (Bhandari, 2014). Corporate scandals during the 1990's created the foundation for corporate governance and subsequently IT governance. Both processes share a close link because each represents the controls that track, evaluate and monitor the revenue performance. The dependency on technology systems in a global economy necessitates effective governance mechanisms that support risk management and compliance requirements in an organization.

According to Henry (2016), there is a positive correlation between logistics information technologies (LIT) and company's performance. This study addresses the inconsistencies and gaps in the literature between theoretical frameworks of LIT and revenue performance of an organization. The findings of this study identify that technical and non-technical organizational factors that influence negative revenue performance (Henry, 2016). The application and development of Information and Communication Technologies (ICT) has a significant effect on many industries, especially in the field of freight distribution and channels related. Ayantoyinbo (2015) examined the impact of ICT on the performance of freight distribution in terms of supply chain, logistics and fleet management. One of the major findings of the research is the impact level of ICT use by freight industries in Lagos and Ogun State which falls into moderate impact on their performance as majority of them only use the low technology for information gathering (Ayantoyinbo, 2015).

Differently, Ratna and Kaur (2016) analyse the effect of logistics information technology on workplaces with individuals and society. This scenario considers as maturation level in the field of digital computing which combine with the use of telecommunications technology in order to link many computers into "what is virtually a very large single network which called as Internet". Author's aim in this study is to examine the effects of technology on various job-related factors such as health and safety, job satisfaction, performance, productivity and work life balance. Findings and data have analysed and found that performance is the most impactful factor by introduction of new technology, followed by job satisfaction, health and safety, productivity and work life balance (Ratna & Kaur, 2016).

Cortes, Serna and Gomez (2013), examine and identify that the technology tools are part of the Intelligent Transportation Systems (ITS) use to improve the performance and safety of transport. It's not only for cargo but also of passengers, in different modes such as air, maritime, rail and road. The authors discover that there is a positive significant result that the intelligent transport systems are the tools to allow transport mobility, safety and productivity to improve and involve of many aspects for logistics service performance purposes (Cortes, Serna, & Gomez, 2013).

Similarly, Farhanghi, Abbaspour and Ghassemi (2013) investigate the effect of logistics information technology

(LIT) on organizational structure and firm performance. The findings revealed that LIT has a positive impact on firm's performance (Farhanghi, Abbaspour, & Ghassemi, 2013). The results of the study show that LIT has a direct effect on organization structure and the findings indicate that information technology helps to the firms to be more flexible in the uncertain environments and to be more openness to learning best practices.

After examining the literature, it is apparent that logistics information technology processes (LIT) is important in ensuring performance measurement. However, the further study and analysis of the variable's synchronization is required as a continuous assessment since logistics information technology processes is a vital factor that change its application and upgrade the dimensions from time to time. Based on the above arguments, this study seeks to propose the following hypothesis:

H3: Logistics information technology (LIT) has significant relationship with organization performance in manufacturing firm.

CHAPTER THREE

Exploration Procedure

Introduction

Chapter three reiterates the research objective and covers the research design and methodology employed to meet the goals of the study. The research design section detailed the population characteristics, sampling frame methodology, sample size and construct details. It will discuss operationalization of the variables examine in this study, describes the questionnaire design for data collection, methods of data collection and the procedures follow in collecting data for this study. The data collection section explores alternatives to obtain the necessary data. The survey instrument section discusses pilot test procedures. The analytical procedures including coverage of the assessment techniques for the psychometric properties of the constructs including descriptive statistics, reliability, validity and the model itself wrap up the chapter.

Research Design

Mono quantitative method were used in this study with combination of various components in a reasonable logical manner so that the research problem is efficiently handled (Creswell & Creswell, 2018). Basically the research questions in this study has done with research design. The nature of this study is based on descriptive study with experimental, survey by questionnaires and variable correlational basis which describe the situations effectively and they do not make predictions; they do not determine cause and effect of the study.

There are three main sections of research design in this study which are the data collection process, measurement and analysis. This research design addresses the characteristics of the population analysed, the sampling method employed and a brief explanation on sample size determination. Conducting surveys is an unbiased approach to make decisions and can collect un-bias survey data and develop sensible decisions based on results analysis. Diversely, the cross-sectional research setting was used as it involves gathering of data at one point in time from the manufacturing firm representatives to achieve the research objectives.

Research Approach

Deduction research approach were selected for this study. Quantitative research is normally associated with a deductive approach (Saunders, Lewis, & Thornhill, 2012). This study is to gather quantitative data from manufacturing firms that operates in Negeri Sembilan state in Malaysia and using these data to test and analyse on the theories developed in previous literatures. The deduction approach or method emphasizes on the need to analyse the relationship between variables, which measured in numerical with usage of statistical techniques. Then the causal approach used to examine and to understand the significant relationship between dependent and independent variables towards organization performance in manufacturing firms.

Research Strategy

In this research, the primary data from feedback in questionnaires are the source of information and questionnaire being as data analysis tool in this study. Survey research strategy were used to collect all the necessary information from respondents from manufacturing firms that operates in Negeri Sembilan.

Population and Sample

The targeted respondent's population for this study are the middle level management team (executives) who directly involve with operational or the managers from top level management of logistics or supply chain division. Respondents will be from the manufacturing firms that operates and located in Negeri Sembilan, Malaysia and selected from the list of companies that registered under Federation of Malaysia Manufacturers (FMM). The FMM membership listing provides a good representation of a cross sectional of the business community with members from manufacturers who being as the targeted industries for this survey.

The research mainly assesses on logistics strategies, organizational structure and logistics information technology of the manufacturing firm in a logistics settings. The respondents from these firms would be the operational specialist, experts and who are knowledgeable about the impact of logistics strategies, organizational structures, as well as how they relate the logistics information technology processes on their organization performance. In targeting a sample of a population, the sound of methodology is very important for interpretation and extension of the research findings.

A random sampling technique were employed in this study. Random sampling of manufacturing firms that listed in the Federation of Malaysia Manufacturers (FMM), Negeri Sembilan increases the likelihood that the sample characteristics are representative of those in the population (McMillan & Schumacher, 2001). The sample size ought to be suitably broad to assess the characteristics of the population adequately to deliver realistic outcomes. The guiding principle based on Saunders, Lewis and Thornhill (2012) and the sample size is adapted as per Table 3.1.

Table 3.1: Sample Size

	Margin of Error (5%)	Margin of Error (1%)
Population (N)	Sample Size (s)	Sample Size (s)
50	44	50
150	108	148
200	132	195
500	217	475
750	254	696
1000	278	906

Source: Saunders, Lewis & Thornhill (2012)

According to the list of companies that register under Federation of Malaysia Manufacturers (FMM), Negeri Sembilan branch for year 2019, there are 179 manufacturing companies are active in the FMM list (*source of information retrieved from https://www.fmm.org.my/Negeri_Sembilan.aspx*). Therefore, 170 respondents been selected to serve as the questionnaire respondents who intend for this research at a 75 percent of confidence level response with minimum required of 132 sample size (Saunders, Lewis, & Thornhill, 2012). Sample size effects the significant results, since larger sample sizes decrease sampling distribution standard error and increasing the sampling distribution around the population parameter.

Instruments and Measurements

This study provides a test of the model described and measure development which requires examination of the literature and feedback from company representatives on the items to identify the correct measures to represent the unobservable variables. This procedure enables refinement of the items to ensure the measures are accurately represent the domain of the concepts.

The first step will be the content assessment or post-instrument inquiry to assess the content of the survey instrument to ensure the relevance of the research questions, the appropriateness of the constructs and the readability of the items. The second phase will be the method or medium assessment to evaluate the ease of use of the web-based survey which relatively being as new approach for data collection via the internet by using Google forms icon.

The items of the variables in the questionnaire is adapt from previous studies related with logistics strategy, organizational structure, logistics information technology and organization performance to go well with the research objectives of the study (Gu, Hung, & Tse, 2008). The questionnaire comprises of 20 items (20 questions related with variables of research topic).

Respondents requested to respond to the statement of the question using a "five-point Likert scale", ranging from 1 which is "strongly disagree" to 5 which means "strongly agree" to record the degree of their assessment and perception on each item. Likert scale is easy for respondents to read, understand and report their perceptions regarding behaviours, attitudes and assessments of research variables. Likert scale being as one of the most commonly used scales and supports in previous studies related to examine the effect of different strategic orientations, organizational structures and LIT on the performance of the organization.

Section A: Demography

This part included with warm up questions about the background of the respondents and eight type of questions were prepared to analyse the details of respondents from manufacturing sector. The respondents have to thick the provided optional answers for item one to six and item seven and eight are subjective question.

Section B: Logistics Strategy

The items for the logistics strategy in this study are from Schellenberg (2013) and Ghiani, Laporte and Musmanno (2013). In all, five items are used to measure logistics strategy on a 5-point Likert scale (refer to Table 3.2). These are statements that describe the degree of logistics strategies and practices in manufacturing firm and the respondents shall indicate how they agree or disagree with each statement based on the scales below.

Table 3.2: Logistics Strategy Scale

No.	Item	Scale				
1.	Primary objective of logistics is to effectively manage activities that results in supply chain, manufacturing and distribution costs	5	4	3	2	1
2.	Logistics functions are managed as a value added system	5	4	3	2	1
3.	Logistics facilitates the management of information flows among channel members (manufacturer, distributors, wholesalers, dealers, retailers and customers)	5	4	3	2	1
4.	Logistics facilitates the coordination of several business units in order to provide competitive customer service	5	4	3	2	1
5.	Logistics facilitates inter-organizational coordination through cooperation and collaboration with dealers or distributors	5	4	3	2	1

Section C: Organizational Structure

The organizational structure scales are adapt from Banerjee and Srivastava (2017), Toriello (2017) and Espino-Rodrı́guez and Gil-Padilla (2015). The below statements describe the degree of centralization or decentralization in manufacturing firm that used in making the following decision and the respondents shall indicate how they agree or disagree with each statement based on the scales below.

Table 3.3: Organizational Structure Scale

No.	Item	Scale				
1.	Less traditional structures are more loosely woven and flexible with the ability to respond quickly to changing business environments	5	4	3	2	1
2.	Achieving alignment and sustaining organizational capacity requires time and critical thinking	5	4	3	2	1
3.	Strategy must continually drive organization structure and people decisions, and the structure and design must reflect and enable effective leadership	5	4	3	2	1
4.	Five elements will create an effective organizational structure: job design, departmentalization, delegation (empowerment), span of control and chain of command	5	4	3	2	1
5.	Organizational realignment involves closing the structural gaps and power distance that impeding organizational performance	5	4	3	2	1

Section D: Logistics Information Technology (LIT)

The items for the logistics information technology processes were adapted from Arthur, Stephen, Wilson and Ronald (2016) and Osayuwamen (2018). These are statements that describe the degree of logistics information technology processes and practices in an organization and the respondents shall indicate how they agree or disagree with each statement based on the scales below.

Table 3.4: Logistics Information Technology Scale

No.	Item	Scale				
1.	Integrating new technology into existing logistic operations can help in increasing customer service, reduce cost and streamline supply chains	5	4	3	2	1
2.	Logistics information systems promote the flexible use and coordination of resources to support knowledge management skills and quick decision making	5	4	3	2	1
3.	Firm and industry has increased the use of Electronic Data Interchange (EDI) standards, integrated inventory system, transportation and warehousing planning system during the past three years	5	4	3	2	1
4.	Logistics information technology (LIT) provide real-time tracking and accurate delivery systems	5	4	3	2	1
5.	The emerging new technologies are creating strategic opportunities for the organizations to build competitive advantages in various functional areas of management	5	4	3	2	1

Section E : Organization Performance

The organization performance scales are adapted from Aloulou (2018), Henry (2016) and Kimani (2015). Respondents asked to evaluate their company's performance on measures in terms of management, customer and employee perspective based on their environments. The below statements describe the perceptual measurement of firm performance using combination of financial, marketing and less traditional measurement on performance of the manufacturing firm and the respondents shall indicate how they agree or disagree with each statement based on the scales below.

Table 3.5: Organization Performance Scale

No.	Item	Scale				
1.	Organization has the ability to meet quoted or anticipated delivery dates on a consistent basis	5	4	3	2	1
2.	Accommodate delivery times, handle difficulties, non-standard orders and handle product modifications upon customer request	5	4	3	2	1
3.	Perform value added services for customers during the warehouse or distribution processes	5	4	3	2	1
4.	Attain the lowest total supply chain cost by achieving high volume output (economy of scale)	5	4	3	2	1
5.	Perceived logistics performance matches with customer expectations and company goals	5	4	3	2	1

Validity and Reliability

Validity is defined as the degree to which the instrument (questionnaire) measures what it is supposed to measure and validity can be evaluate in two ways, either via content validity or construct validity (Creswell & Creswell, 2018). Content validity is a subjective assessment and it is based on personal judgment. Questionnaires will verify and determine based on the judgments from perspective of the experts and specialist from manufacturing firms. While, the construct validity measured by using factor analysis and it can be validated from the questionnaire and verify if the items are loading on the correct factors (Cronbach, 2004).

The first step is to evaluate the variable's descriptive statistics with standard deviations and ranges of responses which could provide insight into the usefulness of the continuous variables in a study. The next step is evaluating the data by assess of univariate and multivariate normality, in order to ensure the proper estimation technique were employed. The items frequencies can use to develop histograms and it is useful in assessing the normality (Saunders, Lewis, & Thornhill, 2012).

Factor analysis will be conducted and once the descriptive statistics are evaluated, then the next step is to assess the reliability of the measures to evaluate the level of random sources of error affecting the values. Reliability evaluates how well similar, but still independent, measures of a single construct act in a comparable manner (Agata, 2015). Cronbach (2004) thoughts on coefficient alpha explains the traditional measure of reliability in empirical research and indicates that an acceptable alpha cut-off to ensure reliability is 0.80 which considered good and at least 0.7 which consider as a deemed acceptable level.

To establish content validity, the literature will examine and determine whether the scale and the items are most representative of the domain of each construct (Banerjee & Srivastava, 2017). Content validity attempts is to capture "what exactly the instrument is measuring", therefore industry professionals will ask to provide feedback regarding the adequacy of the items and the fit of the conceptual definitions of the constructs. An assessment of construct validity, convergent validity, discriminant validity, content validity, and unidimensional will help to provide an answer to this question.

Pilot Test

As the most of the previous studies were carried out in other countries with various dimensions, the questionnaire has to be tested for Malaysian context, in order to prevent misconceptions or misinterpretations of questions and study purpose. Therefore, this study emphasizes on the necessity of pilot testing the instruments that used in the study in order to ensuring the words, phrases and the sequence of questions that are comprehensible for the respondents (Sekaran, 2003). Pilot test were conducted to a group of management representatives or logistics specialists who been requested to help in the development of the questionnaires.

The objective of the process is to seek and ensure that the survey questionnaire is understandable and relevant to the variables that useful in the measurement. A sample of 38 individuals similar to the population of study were selected and determined that the respondents understand the questionnaire and to meet the objective of the study. Based on the response from the 38 respondents, reliability analysis was carried out and the results as shown in Table 3.6 and all items met the required specifications.

Table 3.6: Reliability analysis of variables for pilot test

Variable	Item	Cronbach's Alpha
Organization Performance (OP)	5	0.853
Logistics Strategy (LS)	5	0.881
Organizational Structure (OS)	5	0.786
Logistics Information Technology (LIT)	5	0.912

Data Collection Procedures

Once the questionnaire has been pilot tested and revised, the questionnaire was distributed to the targeted population. The web administrated questions was constructed via Google forms software application. According to Dillman (1999), self-administered survey is more effective, reliable and influences the level of satisfactory responses from the respondents. Moreover, completed questionnaires can be collected in a short period of time. Data in this study collected through indirect interaction via e-mail by using self-administered questionnaires. Respondents were invited to access the questionnaire via hyperlink and were used one-time survey strategy. The purpose of the research and the instructions to complete the questionnaire are well explained.

A total of 170 sets of questionnaires been e-mailed to the respondents who are from various manufacturing organization's (executive level and above) that appear in the list of companies that registered under FMM Negeri

Sembilan, Malaysia. Data file was generated once respondents completed the questionnaire. The file was automatically stored in Google forms database and it was retrieved in excel spreadsheet. Then the data transferred to IBM SPSS software version 25 for further statistical analysis purposes.

Data Analysis Method

To establish a level of confidence in measurements, the data obtained from questionnaire were employed and examined in SPSS software for descriptive statistics and then evaluate the reliability and internal consistency of the measures along with an assessment of the validity. Descriptive, reliability, correlation and multiple regression analysis were carried out to examine the hypothesis testing.

Data Screening

Data screening is a process to ensure the accuracy of data and a key process that would not produce distort correlation (Tabachnick & Fidell, 2007). Data screening process were conducted through the detection of missing value analysis and assessment of outliers (either with skewness or kurtosis - square root, inverse or using logarithms in SPSS software).

Descriptive Analysis

Descriptive Analysis is to show the situation analysis that can be summarized into useful data that can be used, presented in frequency and can represent the variables. Descriptive analysis also measures of mean, standard deviation and variance of the data that have been collected, to figure out the central tendency and describe the essential characteristics of variables and results.

Reliability Test

Reliability test is to test the accuracy and reliability of the data collected. Cronbach's Alpha is used in this research to measure how strong reliability in the item grouped for each variable (Saunders, Lewis, & Thornhill, 2012). The Table 3.7 shows the value rules of the reliability value.

Table 3.7: Cronbach's Alpha Coefficient Value

Alpha Coefficient Range	Strength
0.0 - < 0.6	Poor
0.6 - < 0.7	Moderate
0.7 - < 0.8	Good
0.8 - < 0.9	Very Good
0.9 - 1.0	Excellent

Source: (Zikmund, Babin, Carr & Griffin, 2010).

Pearson's Correlation Analysis

The reason to use "Pearson's Correlation Analysis" is to analysis the strength of the linear relationship between two variables (Saunders, Lewis, & Thornhill, 2012). The range of person Correlation Analysis is between -1 to +1, it would result in to show whether both have a negative or positive relationship. If the data showing result of '+1', which mean both have a perfect positive relationship; if the result shows

'-1', that mean both have a perfect negative relationship; if the result shows is in '0', that mean both have no relationship. Similarly, if the p-value is less than alpha value of 0.05, there is significant relationship between the independent and dependent variables.

Linear Regression Analysis

Linear regression analysis is the method used to find out how dependent variable and independent variable are related and to estimate the qualifying impact of each factor (Saunders, Lewis, & Thornhill, 2012). R^2 value were used to explain the strength of relationship between both independent variables and dependent variable. When the value of R^2 is high, it shows that the independent variable will have higher influence to the dependent variable. The relationship between independent and dependent variables must be linear. If non-linear relationship exists, the actual strength of the relationships will be underestimates and the linearity can be examined by the residual plots. Once the measurement model is determined, the next step is to use the structural model to assess the hypotheses associates with the research questions and must be evaluate on the goodness of fit indices.

Summary

Chapter three describe the research design and methodology that employed to assess the stated research objectives. This research is a descriptive study by using a survey method to collect data. Research framework has formed based on BRV theory and three hypotheses were developed. The chapter discusses about the methodology that adapted in collecting data and techniques for analyses of data. Moreover, this chapter provide elaborations on the targeted population, sampling frame and the justification of the respondent's sample size. In addition, this chapter also explain the instruments that used, based on the relevant literature review. Apart from that, this chapter discuss the research questions and model constructs along with identifying the procedures necessary to accomplish a thorough evaluation of the model. This study is a quantitative research since the research design, approach and paradigm are aligned with quantitative research style. Primary data is the source of the information that collected from online questionnaire response. Chapter four will provides details of the data analysis and findings of this study.

CHAPTER FOUR

Discovery Facts

Introduction

This chapter presents and describes results of the analysis performed in this study and discusses the data collection process, response rate, methods of data cleaning and screening process. Tests for normality, reliability, descriptive statistics, hypotheses testing, co-relation analysis, multiple collinearity, multiple regression and factor analysis also were conducted. This study aimed to determine the effect of the logistics factors on organization performance among the manufacturing firms in Negeri Sembilan. Three hypotheses were formed, tested and the results are discussed in the following session.

Descriptive Statistics of Variables

A total number of 170 questionnaires were distributed to the manufacturing firms in Negeri Sembilan either using postal mail or online Google Forms linked survey method. In total, 150 respondents have answered the questionnaire that distributed and 136 are valid and the balance 14 considered as invalid responses due to incomplete form. The data were collected within three months period from April to June, 2019.

Demographic Profile

The demographic characteristics of respondents are described in Table 4.1. After the data screening, 14 incomplete responses were deleted and the total valid responses for the final analysis are 136.

Table 4.1: Respondents Demographic Composition

Variable	Category	Frequency	Percentage (%)
Gender	Male	83	61.03
	Female	53	38.97
Age group	25 and below	3	2.20
	26 - 30	14	10.30
	31 – 40	27	19.85
	41 – 50	66	48.53
	Above 50	26	19.12
Ethnicity	Malay	37	27.21
	Chinese	42	30.88
	Indian	54	39.70
	Other	3	2.21
Educational details	Diploma	16	11.76
	Bachelor Degree	66	48.54
	Master Degree	45	33.09
	PhD	9	6.62
Job Position	Top Management	40	29.41
	Senior Management/ Managers	54	39.71
	Senior Executive/Middle management	40	29.41
	Non-executive/ operational	2	1.47
Experience in present organization (years)	Less than 1	10	7.35
	1 – 3	23	16.91
	4 – 6	34	25.00
	7 – 9	43	31.62
	More than 10	26	19.12
Total		136	100

Among the total respondents, males represented 61.03 percent (83) of the sample population, while female constituted of 38.97 percent (53). The majority of respondents with 48.53 percent are from age group between 41-50 years old and 19.85 percent from age group of 31 to 40 years. Only 2.20 percent of minority respondents are from age group of below 25 years old.

The majority of respondents are Indians (39.70 percent), followed by Chinese (30.88 percent) and Malay (27.21 percent). Thus, it can be concluded that majority of the manufacturers' representatives in this study were local Malaysians and most of them are from adult's category within the age group of 31-40 years old (19.85 percent) and 41-50 years old (48.53 percent). Apart from that, most of the respondents has obtained tertiary education either Bachelor degrees or Master's degrees (in total 111 respondents) in respective fields such as Supply Chain Management, Business Administration and Economy. Therefore, it can be concluded that based on the findings, the management representatives from manufacturing firms in Negeri Sembilan are highly educated and well experienced in their field.

Most of the respondents are being as the decision makers in their respective fields such as Supply Chain division, Logistics department or from Warehouse and 54 of them are being as senior management/managers while 40 respondents are from top management of the company. On top of that, majority of them are the senior staffs in their present firm whereby 31.62 percent (43) are between 7-9 years, 25 percent (34) of respondents are between 4-6 years and 19.12 percent (26) of respondents with more than 10 years. The age group of 25 and below, other ethnicity and non-executive/operational positioners are under-represented in this study due to lack of experience, less knowledge factor in respective field, only few foreign representatives that worked and represent the Multi National Company (MNC), due to low authority level in order to evaluate the company performances and less involve in decision making processes.

The aim and the purpose is to analyse the effect of logistics strategy, organizational structure and logistics information technology (LIT) on organization performance of manufacturing firms that located in Negeri Sembilan state. The manufacturing firm's respondents who participated in this study were comprised of several manufacturing sectors that operates in Negeri Sembilan, Malaysia. Majority of respondents were from Electrical, Electronic and Appliances, 22 firms (16.8 percent), 19 are from Chemical sector (13.97 percent) and 17 (12.5 percent) responses from Food and Beverage sector. Respondents from Rubber and Plastics with Others sectors are only 16 in total. The complete list of the respondent's type according to the sector is presented in Table 4.2.

Table 4.2: Nature of Business

Nature of Business	Frequency	Percentage (%)
Textiles and Apparels	10	7.35
Wood and Furniture	13	9.56
Food and Beverages	17	12.5
Chemicals	19	13.97
Transport Equipment	13	9.56
Metallurgical Supplies	14	10.29
Electrical, Electronics and Appliances	22	16.18
Rubber and Plastics	7	5.15
Engineering	12	8.82
Others	9	6.62
Total	136	100

The annual gross sales range, 11 firms (8.09 percent) earn more than RM10 million annually, while 29 firms (21.32 percent) earns an annual gross revenue of in between RM 5 to 10 million. In average, 63.23 percent of respondents are earned more than RM 1 Million as an annual gross sale in Negeri Sembilan state. The full figures are being presented in Table 4.3 as below:

Table 4.3: Annual Gross Sales

Annual Gross Sales	Frequency	Percentage (%)
Less than RM500,000	18	13.24
RM500,000 - RM1,000,000	32	23.53
RM1,000,001 - RM5,000,000	46	33.82
RM5,000,001 - RM10,000,000	29	21.32
Above RM10,000,000	11	8.09
Total	136	100

Descriptive Statistics

Descriptive statistics obtained to examine the average scores for each independent and dependent variable applied in this study. The variables are based on five-point Likert scale ranging from one, as minimum which means 'Strongly disagree' to five as a maximum which means 'Strongly Agree'. The means and standard deviation of all variables in this study are displayed in Table 4.4.

Variable	N	Mean	Standard Deviation	Skewness	Kurtosis
OP	136	3.83	0.743	-1.349	0.871
LS	136	3.89	0.771	-0.736	1.716
OS	136	3.83	0.761	-1.481	0.723
LIT	136	3.91	0.776	-0.435	1.118

Table 4.4: Descriptive Analysis of independent and dependent variables

On a five-point Likert scale, the mean score for 'Organization Performance' was 3.83 while the standard deviation at 0.743. The mean score for the organization performance can be classified as relatively high. According to Morrison, Manion and Cohen, (2011) "a mean score of 4.21 and above is considered as "very high", a mean score of between 3.41 and 4.20 is considered as "high", while mean score of 3.41 and below is classified as "moderate". The results indicate that the manufacturing companies in Negeri Sembilan, Malaysia were relatively highly performance oriented which supported with logistics system.

The independent variable 'Logistics Information Technology (LIT)' has the highest mean scores with 3.91 whereas the lowest mean score of 3.82 obtained by independent variable 'Organizational Structure', but still categorised as high rating scores (Morrison, Manion, & Cohen, 2011). These indicated that, respondents in general have positive attitude and significant reflection of factors that affect the organization performance from the logistics perspective. The normality of distribution of data been examined to a certain extend by the skewness and kurtosis values for each variable within the limitation of between -2 and + 2.0 (Chua, 2006).

Reliability Analysis

Reliability test is conducted to ensure the study fulfils its expected aims and hypothesis and also to ensure the results are due to the study and measure the consistency. Table 4.5 shows the Cronbach's Alpha for all variables based on the data collected from 136 valid responses.

Table 4.5: Cronbach's Alpha for Reliability Analysis of variables

Variable	Item	Cronbach's Alpha
Organization Performance (OP)	5	0.977
Logistics Strategy (LS)	5	0.971
Organizational Structure (OS)	5	0.968
Logistics Information Technology (LIT)	5	0.969

5 statements (item) were designed for each variable to analyse the organization performance as a reflection of logistics perspective in manufacturing firms in Negeri Sembilan. All variables have Cronbach's Alpha of more than 0.90 and close to 1.0, which ensure and confirmed the reliability level at high. Therefore, it can be concluded that the combination of statements that generated for each variable tested has generated stable results or shows the consistency of the measurement about organization performance with similar studies (Saunders, Lewis, & Thornhill, 2012). Thus, each variable is reliable to determine the relationship between the independent variables to the organization performance among the manufacturing firms in Negeri Sembilan.

Pearson Correlation Analysis

Before presenting and testing the hypotheses with multiple regression, Pearson Correlation Analysis were computed between performance and each of the independent variable (logistics strategy, organizational structure and logistics information technology) and dependent variable (organization performance). The bivariate analysis mode conducted to identify the association and strength between these variables. According to (Pallant, 2007), correlation coefficient from ±.1 to ±.29 is small; a correlation coefficient from ±.30 to ±.49 is medium; and a correlation coefficient from ±.50 to ±1.0 is large. The results of the Pearson correlation analysis are shown in Table 4.6.

Table 4.6: Pearson Correlation Analysis

Variable	Correlation, r	P-value
Correlation with Organization Performance (OP)		
Logistics Strategy (LS)	0.883	0
Organizational Structure (OS)	0.867	0
Logistics Information Technology (LIT)	0.868	0

The results show that the independent variables are positively correlated with 0.883 (LS), 0.867 (OS) and 0.868 (LIT) respectively with 0 p-value, which is less than the alpha value of 0.05. Therefore, it can be concluded that all independent variables are significantly related with dependent variable (OP). The results also show that there is strong relationship between independent variable with organization performance of manufacturing firms.

Multiple Collinearity Analysis

Multiple Collinearity Analysis is further extended to analyse and measure the relationship between independent variables for organization performance. Table 4.7 executed the correlation matrix between independent variable of logistics strategy, organizational structure and logistics information technology (LIT).

Table 4.7: Multiple Collinearity Analysis

Variables	OP	LS	OS	LIT
Organization Performance (OP)	1.000			
Logistics Strategy (LS)	0.598**	1.000		
Organizational Structure (OS)	0.396**	0.284*	1.000	
Logistics Information Technology (LIT)	0.421*	0.351**	0.102**	1.000

** Correlation is significant at 0.01 level (2 tailed)
* Correlation is significant at 0.05 level (1 tailed)

The correlation results show that the three independent variables of logistics strategy, organizational structure and logistics information system (LIT) were positively and significantly correlated with the dependent variable of organization performance. Hair, Babin, Anderson and Rolph (2009) argued that correlation analysis only gives a clear picture of the association, strength and the nature of the relationship between variables. It cannot be used as a valid technique to analyse the predictor nature of the variables in the relationship of two or more variables. Therefore, to examine the effect of logistics strategy, organizational structure and logistics information system (LIT) processes on organization performance and to reveal any variance that may be caused by these variables, multiple collinearity analysis was used to examine the relationship between all variables used in this study.

Based on the findings, logistics strategy to be strongly perceived logistics information technology (r=0.351) and organizational strategy (r=0.284). Similarly, organizational structure has relatively perceived or correlated with logistics information technology (r=0.102). In addition, multicollinearity enables to identify which of the independent variables has more predictive power towards the dependent variable. The outcome of the multiple regression analysis gave answers to the first three research objectives as well as the hypotheses in this study. The Variance Inflation Factor (VIF) is determined and detect multicollinearity as shown in Table 4.8.

Table 4.8: Multi-Collinearity Analysis for independent variables

Variable	Tolerance	VIF
Logistics Strategy (LS)	0.876	1.821
Organizational Structure (OS)	0.712	1.120
Logistics Information Technology (LIT)	0.927	1.462

Based on the theory, multi-collinearity statistics used to check construct validity on all of the instrument scales and the results would be used to primarily determine the dimensionality of constructs. According to Barlett (1954), collinearity statistic should be at a minimum of 0.6 (Kaiser, 1974). The results show that the values are more than 0.7 which is consider as "good" and the VIF value within the range of 1 to 2 which means within the acceptance level and the results of regression analysis proved that there is correlation between all independent variables with organization performance.

Multiple Regression Analysis

Multiple Regression Analysis is a powerful technique used for predicting the unknown value of a variable from the known value of two or more variables which also called as the predictors. In this study, regression analysis used to understand the strength of the relationship between variables. The regression procedure results in a beta weight (β) which provides a useful interpretation of the relationship between independent and dependent variables. The (β) value, which may be either positive or negative, indicates the amount of increase or decrease in a dependent variable for one unit of difference in the independent variable.

The regression output also provides the correlation coefficient (r), coefficient of determination (R^2) and adjusted coefficient of determination (adjusted R^2), both of which indicate how well an independent variable predicts the dependent variable. The coefficient of determination (R^2) represents the degree of variance accounted for by the independent variable. In other words, the R square (R^2) indicates the percentage of the total variation in the dependent variable values attributable to, or explained by, the independent variable in a regression equation (Mendenhall & Sincich, 1989). The F value is a criterion to evaluate the overall usefulness of the regression model in analysing, predicting or explaining the variation in the dependent variable (Bohrnstedt & Knoke, 1992).

In this study, the relationship is statistically significant if the value of F is larger than .05 (Prob > F). Multiple regression analysis was conducted for independent variables; logistics strategy, organizational structure and logistics information technology and dependent variable; organization performance by using SPSS software, version 25. The main objective is to determine the significant relationship between the three independent variables and the dependent variable. In addition, it enables to identify which of the independent variables has more predictive power towards the dependent variable. The outcome of the multiple regression analysis gave answers to research objectives as well as the hypotheses in this study (Table 4.9, 4.10, and 4.11).

Table 4.9: Regression Model Summary

Model	R	R^2	Adjusted R^2	Std. Error of the Estimate
1	.473[a]	.491	.133	.35643

Table 4.10: ANOVA (Significance of Regression Model)

Model 1	Sum of Squares	Df	Mean Square	F	Sig
Regression	15.321	3	3.864	19.221	.000
Residual	53.483	133	.179		
Total	68.804	136			

Table 4.11: Multiple Regressions Analysis

Model 1	Standardized Coefficients Beta	T	Sig.
Logistics Strategy	.494	6.848	.000*
Organizational Structure	.293	4.770	.000*
Logistics Information Technology	.339	5.518	.000*

*Significance at *$p < 0.01$*

In order to test the above hypothesis, multiple regression is performed. Based on results from the table above, it can be concluded that R^2 of 0.473 which means 47.30% variance in the organization performance in manufacturing firms via independent variable. H^1 is accepted since the p-value is less than alpha value of 0.05 and determine the regression model is good. Model 1 also reflect there is positive relationship among all variables and significant relationship between logistics strategy (LS) (t=6.848, p-value=.000), organizational structure (OS) (t=4.770, p-value=.000) and logistics information technology (LIT) (t=5.518, p-value=.000). The strength and the significance relationship of independent variables with organization performance are strong and positive for logistics strategy (β=.494), organizational structure (β=.293) and logistics information technology (LIT) (β=.339).

These results supported the hypotheses H^1, H^2 and H^3 and there are significant relationship between all variables. The analyses also show the three predictors accounted for 19.7 percent of the variance in organization performance (R^2=.491, F=19.221 and p=.000). Apart from that, the coefficients for all predictor variables were positive. The findings indicate that a change in logistics strategy results in 0.494 change in organization performance, a change in organizational structure results in a change of 0.293 in organization performance while a change in logistics information technology results in 0.339 change in organization performance.

Hypothesis Testing

This section will address each of the stated hypotheses in the study. Multiple regression analysis was performed to assess the direct and indirect relationships within the proposed model and the stated hypotheses.

H1: Logistics strategy has significant relationship with organization performance in manufacturing firm. Therefore, H^1 is accepted.
H2: Organizational structure has significant relationship with organization performance in manufacturing firm. Therefore, H^2 is accepted.
H3: Logistics Information Technology (LIT) has significant relationship with organization performance in manufacturing firm. Therefore, H^3 is accepted.

Summary

This chapter presented results of the analyses performed in this study. Out of 170 questionnaires distributed, only 136 consider as valid response. Based on the valid responses, it can be concluded that all variables are positively related and significant among one to another. The topic discussed includes common method variance, the means and standard deviations of all variables of study, the correlation and the regressions analyses on the direct relationships among the variables. The results revealed there are direct significant relationships between the independent variables (logistics strategy, organizational structure and logistics information technology) and dependent variable (organization performance). The discussion on these findings as well as the conclusions and recommendations will be in Chapter Five.

CHAPTER FIVE

Dialogue and Decision

Introduction

This chapter provides discussion on the findings that have been presented in the preceding chapter. The chapter draws detailed discussion on the theoretical perspectives of variables and also connects them to the previous studies found in the literature. The organization of the chapter will be as follows: First, the chapter provides the recapitulation of the key findings, to be followed by the review of demographic profiles of the respondents as well as the descriptive presentation of means scores of all variables of study. It will proceed with the examination and discussion on the results of each three hypotheses tested in this study. It later provides the theoretical and practical implications of the study. Lastly, the chapter addresses the limitations of study as well as provides some suggestions for future study or further researches.

Recapitulation of Study

This study examined the direct relationships between three independent variables; logistics strategic, organizational structure and logistics information technology (LIT), and a dependent variable; organization performance of manufacturing firms in Negeri Sembilan. Overall, the study has succeeded in advancing the current understanding of knowledge factors that affecting directly the organization performance of manufacturing firms in Negeri Sembilan, Malaysia from logistics perspectives.

This study employed a structured survey questionnaire in the data collection and the sample population was the manufacturing firms that registered in FMM Negeri Sembilan, Malaysia. Top management, managers or company representatives were chosen as the organization representative because they are usually involved in decision making process of day-to-day running of the businesses and therefore, they are in a better position to provide the needed, available and accurate information about their firms.

A total of 170 firms that appeared in the sampling frame were randomly selected and sent with the survey questionnaires. Both mail and e-mail methods were utilized. A total of 150 responses were returned and after the cleaning process, only 136 were accepted for the final analysis. The data were keyed into the SPSS software version 25, and descriptive and inferential analyses were conducted. Principal component analysis (PCA) was also conducted to determine the construct validity of the instruments. The factor analysis results indicated the unidimensional constructs for logistics strategy, organizational structure and logistics information technology (LIT). All the three hypotheses (H1, H2 & H3) were tested simultaneously using multiple regressions. All hypothesis as predicted, has significant relationship with organization performance and supported with positive results.

Discussion of findings

In general, respondents have response positively towards how the logistics system in a firm affect the organization performance; fundamentally from logistics perspective. As a result, the study shows that the organization performance generated positive reflections with an average value of 3.83 out of the range of 1 (low performance) to 5 (high performance). The indicators for logistics strategy, organizational structure and logistics information system (LIT) also with high mean of 3.89, 3.83 and 3.91 respectively. This indicate that the three main independent variables play an important role and create great opportunity in order to meet targeted organization performance in order to achieve company goals.

On the other hand, these being as a proof that logistics system and the strategy, logistics organization structure and information technology being as anchor for a sustainable manufacturing company that compete in rival market in Negeri Sembilan. Among the significant independent variables, the strength of the relationship of independent variables with organization performance of manufacturing firm is logistics strategy (t=6.848, p-value=.000 and β=.494), followed by logistics information technology (t=5.518, p-value=.000 and β=.339) and lastly is the organizational structure (t=4.770, p-value=.000 and β=.293).

Direct effect of Logistics Strategy on Organization Performance

This study examined the direct relationship between logistics strategy on organization performance of manufacturing firms in Negeri Sembilan. The logistics strategy refers to activities that results in supply chain performance (in manufacturing and distribution), the value-added system, information's that flows among channel members, competitive customer services and collaboration with dealers or distributors.

In the context of this study, organization performance conceptualises as the ability to meet promised delivery dates and customer requests, perform value added services in distribution processes, achieving high volume output and meet customer expectations and company goals either financially or non-financially and both. Therefore, the primary objective of logistics is to effectively manage the key activities that results in supply chain performances, manufacturing output and distribution costs (Ittner, Larcker & Randall, 2003). The logistics facilitates the management with information flows among channel members such as manufacturer, distributors, wholesalers, dealers, retailers and customers. Similarly, logistics has facilitated the coordination of several business units in order to provide competitive customer service (Wu, 2018). Thus, logistics also facilitates the inter-organizational coordination through cooperation and collaboration with dealers or distributors. Therefore, it can be concluded that logistics functions are managed the operational activities as a value-added system in manufacturing firms (Kyengo, 2014).

These two variables are combined into a unidimensional management strategy in achieving organizational goals. It is hypothesized that when logistics strategy is being fully practiced in the manufacturing firm, it will improve the performance and strengthening competitiveness in the organization. Performance was measured subjectively by self-reporting based on the growth rate, sales growth relative to competitors, employment growth rate, market value growth, gross profit, return on assets, return on investments and overall company performance. Past studies has identified the significance of logistics strategies being as predictor to improve the overall performance of the firms but its inconclusive findings of the contributions towards manufacturing firms in local Malaysian companies and therefore were triggered for more investigation to be conducted on this relationship (Rehman, 2017 and Tan, Ng, Fong, Chong, & Sukumaran, 2016). However, Gokus (2008), and Ittner, Larcker and Randall (2003) highlighted that greater strategic change in poorer performing firms than in better performing firms.

The result of the regression analysis showed that the relationship between logistics strategy and organization performance of manufacturing firm was significant. The further analysis was conducted via correlation and multiple regression analysis. The analysis shows that there is significant and positive relationship between logistics strategy with organization performance. The positive results show that the respondents feel more positive and gain benefits from implementation, adaptation and monitoring of strategies in logistics system in order for better organization performance. This positive relationship has confirmed the findings from previous literature by researchers Schellenberg (2013) and Wu (2018).

Direct effect of Organization Structure on Organization Performance

This study also examined the direct relationship between organization structure and performance of a manufacturing firm. In this study, organizational structure in logistics settings refers to less traditional structures with ability to change business environments, enforce effective leadership, time management, critical thinking and organizational realignment by closing the structural gaps and power distance (Nwonu, Agbaeze & Obi-Anike, 2017). To capture a more complete understanding of organizational structure, it is subdivided into three specific dimensions whereby consists of centralization, formalization and specialization (Toriello, 2017). While, organization performance is ability to meet promised delivery dates and customer requests, perform value added services during distribution processes, achieving high volume output, meet customer expectations and company goals either financially or non-financially and both (Schellenberg, 2013).

The past studies were concluded that the relationship between organizational structure and performance of an organization is not clear and needs further study and examination (Banerjee & Srivastava, 2017; Espino-Rodrı́guez & Gil-Padilla, 2015). Thus, it is hypothesized that organization structure can have a positive influence to firm's performance in the long run. Findings in this study shows that the organizational structure also significant positively and influence the organization performance of manufacturing firms in Negeri Sembilan. The findings indicate that the decentralization structure, highly intense and influential system is associates with greater system success in terms of both externally perceive outcomes as well as the ability to improve existing operations.

Additionally, the results denote the effect of improving operations and perception of organization performance of the firm as a manufacturer in rival market (Smith, 2007). Put differently as per regression analysis, it means that an improvement in organizational structure will leads to a corresponding increase in organization performance in manufacturing firms. When leaders or managers in a manufacturing firm practice effective leadership, formal allocation of duties, responsibilities, roles and the administrative protocols to control and integrate work related activities they can achieve long-term success and overall firm performance will be positively enhanced. The more an organization engages in structural practices, the greater the firm's performance (Banerjee & Srivastava, 2017).

Other similar leadership studies which are in agreement with the finding of this study include studies on organizational structure and improved the firm's performance (Toriello, 2017; Banerjee & Srivastava, 2017; Nchorbuno, Shafiwu & Ayamga 2017). All these researchers advocated that certain type of organizational structure practiced by the manufacturing firms can bring positive results to their firm's performance either financially or non-financially or both.

Similarly, the five elements that will create an effective organizational structure in manufacturing firms are job design (structural functioning), departmentalization, job delegation (empowerment), span of control and chain of command (centralization and decentralization). As a conclusion, the strategy must continually drive organization structure and people decisions in order to gain extensive performance, and the structure and design must reflect and enable effective leadership.

Direct effect of Logistics Information Technology (LIT) on Organization Performance

This study further examined the direct relationship between logistics information technology (LIT)) and organization performance in manufacturing firm in Negeri Sembilan, Malaysia. The revolution of Information Technology in industries especially in manufacturing sectors permits an integration in logistics systems and improved information sharing with communication abilities by improving the performance of an organization. Apparently, communication technology highly contributed to the development of logistics services with organization performance (Tang, Wong, & Foon, 2018). Thus, it is hypothesized that when logistics information technology (LIT) processes is being practiced in the manufacturing firm, it will improve performance and strengthening the competitiveness in the industry.

In addition, LIT is more specified as integrating new technology, integrated inventory system, transportation and warehousing planning system, creating strategic opportunities by real-time tracking and accurate delivery systems. After examining the past studies, it is apparent that logistics information technology (LIT) is important in ensuring organization performance measurement (Bhandari, 2014). However, a further study and analyse the synchronization is required as a continuous assessment since logistics information technology is a vital factor that change its application and upgrade the dimensions from time to time (Ratna & Kaur, 2016). The result of the regression analysis showed that the relationship between logistics information technology (LIT) to be significant and postively related with organization performance of manufacturing firms.

Findings revealed that integrating new technology into existing logistic operations, help in increasing customer service, reduce the distribution and delivery system cost, and streamline supply chains processes. The right approach to digitizing supply chains integrates suitable leading-edge technologies with revamped operations (Cortes, Serna, & Gomez, 2013). The results show that many managers are familiar with the basic transformation approach whereby established a vision for the future supply chain, assessing the supply chain's current state and developing a transformation road map. As a result, most of the firms largely focused on improvements in three area; streamlining transactional activities such as those involved in end-to-end planning, supporting major operations such as warehouse management system (WMS), real-time tracking and accurate delivery systems, and sharpening the analysis on which decisions are based (Farhanghi, Abbaspour, & Ghassemi, 2013).

In the literature show overwhelming support for the significant and positive contribution of logistics information technology (LIT) processes on organization performance of manufacturing firms. However, based on findings in questionnaire, there are few company managers or representatives feel that LIT not fully integrated and could not affect directly the organization performance from the logistics settings and it has sync with how it has mentioned by Ayantoyinbo (2015) and Bhandari (2014). However, most of the respondent identified that logistics information technology is the most critical factor that can help the manufacturing firms in Negeri Sembilan to achieve sustainability and competitive advantage in the markets.

Implications of the Study

This study provided insights on organization performances of multiple manufacturing firms that operating in Negeri Sembilan, Malaysia. The study was able to contribute to the employers and body of logistics system as it investigated the direct relationships between the logistics support system factors, namely; logistics strategy, organizational structure, logistics information technology (LIT) and organization performance where no known similar research were done among big or small manufacturing firms that operate in Negeri Sembilan, Malaysia. Thus, these findings have both theoretical and practical implications.

Theoretical and Managerial Implications

The findings demonstrated the importance of logistics system settings factors in determining the success of many firms especially the manufacturing sectors. This study extended similar studies conducted earlier by Aloulou (2018), Angappa, Nachiappan and Thanos (2015), Yavuz and Deligonul (2017), Schellenberg (2013) and Kimani (2015) who found significant and positive contributions of all the three factors on company success. Schellenberg (2013) and Thanos (2015) developed the instruments and tested among the successful manufacturing companies in Canada and US while Yavuz and Deligonul (2017) replicated the study among successful European manufacturers. Thus, this study contributed to the literature by extending it to logistics system perspective on manufacturing firms in a developing industrial based country like Malaysia and focus specifically in Negeri Sembilan state.

In addition, the findings generally confirmed and contradicted the existence of positive and significant effect of the three logistics system factors, namely logistics structure, organizational structure and logistics information technology (LIT) on organization performance in the manufacturing sector in Negeri Sembilan. Thus, it advances and strengthens the theoretical view by confirming and contradicting previous findings on the three logistics system factors as important drivers for achieving higher performance.

To satisfy the customers, the manager or CEO of the company should continue to have employees' development and improving on their service quality characteristics such as provide better service after sales and empowerment which would make an increase in service quality, and improve the organization performance. Responsiveness and flexibility also one of the important factors in an organization such as to provide better choices for customer to choose for and quick respond with the customer order processing. Besides that, company should continue to look for logistics provider that in low cost and look for the material or products provider that in reliable and makes sure all the goods they deliver is without damage.

Besides these three factors, the manager or CEO of the company in Negeri Sembilan, should not avoid to look into different approaches that would affect the business performance of the manufacturing firm. The management of the organization should always sensitive with the changes of the business environment especially in logistics, supply chain the activities that involved in and continuously make improvements that based on the need of the customer in order to enhanced sustainability in the rival market in Negeri Sembilan.

Practical Implications

This study identified that significant relationships exist between logistics strategies and organization performance, organizational structure and firm's performance and, between logistics information technology (LIT) and organization performance of manufacturing firms in Negeri Sembilan. These findings could be useful for owner or managers of manufacturing companies to apply the types of strategies to be employed in managing the business in order to achieve higher level of performance. They can do the self-assessment to improve their cognitive skills to the expected level as well as having a good and proper logistics systems that would help in the company decision-making process from logistics perspective. Sustainability and growth of these manufacturing firms in Negeri Sembilan, Malaysia greatly depends on such factors as the ever-changing business environment, the business strategy, internal resources, leadership and management practices.

Empirical evidence also suggests that certain resources of the firm that are valuable, rare, inimitable and non-substitutable are able to create competitive advantage. Thus, owners or the managers should give more emphasis on the growth and development of manufacturing firms by incorporating the three logistics system factors, that is, organizational structure, logistics strategy and logistics information technologies (LIT) to create efficiency, competitiveness and achieve sustainability. Finally, this study can help manufacturing sector owners or managers and policy makers to develop good technical strategies for the business development, gain competitive advantage, improve performance, highly competitive and ever changing business environments in Negeri Sembilan.

The findings of this study provided a deep understanding on how certain logistics system factors can enhance performance of manufacturing firms in Negeri Sembilan, Malaysia. These could be beneficial to agencies involved such as SME's Corporations, Malaysian Investment Development Authority (MIDA), Malaysia Logistics Supply Chain Association (MLSCA), Malaysia Productivity Corporation (MPC) and Ministry of International Trade and Industry (MITI). The findings of this study could also provide a road map for the policy makers and practitioners. As Malaysia focusing on exporting goods especially electrical and electronic (E&E) products, food and beverage, and semi processed products, the government should encourage more manufacturing companies to grow and continue to enhance the export activities, not just only focus in subsidies and tax relieves, but try to lower down the risks of being taken by the local manufacturers especially in Negeri Sembilan and improve logistics infrastructures and logistics transformation process.

Limitations of Study

This study has few methodological limitations. First, it would be the time constraint and due to the requirement, the study has to be complete within five months of time period from the committed date. Therefore, there are many things could not able to cover and the study mainly focus on manufacturing firms in Negeri Sembilan, rather than the whole Malaysia or any other sectors. Due to this, the impact of the factors that affect the performance of the manufacturing firms will not able to reflect the real situation as in whole Malaysia or all sectors. It would be more interesting if the sector inclusive of those services industry, various distribution channels and other business performing related sectors.

Secondly, the study also relied mainly on self-reports of the respondents. There is no way to check the accuracy of data as no secondary sources were available. In this study, the samples could not represent the population as whole sector because the respondents are more inclined towards age group of 31-50 who holding higher position or being as decision makers in the respective firm. On the other hand, although the surveys were addressed to the manufacturing firm's managers or company representatives, some may simply assign to a subordinate to response, who may not have been well-versed on the logistics system, strategy and the organization performance.

Lastly, this study used subjective measures to determine business performance and they may not explain the actual performance of the manufacturing firms. The best measurement of business performance is always objective measures; however, subjective perceptions of performance have been found to correlate well with objective measures (Baiyi & Fan, 2011).

Recommendations for Future Research

This study has provided an insight on the relationships among logistics factors and organization performance of manufacturing firms that operating in Negeri Sembilan, Malaysia. Despite some limitations, many future research opportunities have emerged throughout the progressive work of this study. Firstly, the subjects for this study focused on logistics or supply chain system and it was limited to those categorise as manufacturing sector that operate in Negeri Sembilan state. The findings of this study may not be generalized to other business sectors in Malaysia or can be expend to other specifications such as more depth to SME's corporation and etc. Thus, a larger sample of organizations by many other sectors might show different patterns. Therefore, encouraged the future researcher have to take some time and effort to have a target respondent from whole country or more states in Malaysia, to have a more accurate data in the research.

Secondly, the data were obtained from the managers or company representatives, who were considered the top person in each firm. They would have the most influence over how decisions were made at each of these firms. It would be useful to obtain a broader sample of operational executives and perhaps even lower ranked employees in future studies. This would minimize any potential bias in the data resulting from the level of informants. Furthermore, it would be interesting to compare perceptions of employees at different levels and accountable for differences in perceptions, if any.

Finally, this study used subjective and self-reported measures of organization performance. This might reflect the degree of self-confidence of respondents when measuring their own performance. Although subjective perceptions of performance have been found to correlate well with objective measures, future research could benefit from the use of more objective measures or a combination of perceptual and objective data to provide reliable conclusions on the performance construct. Interviews and live audit with respondents could be carry out for in-depth understanding of the main determinants to obtain extensive organization performance results.

CONCLUSION

This study investigated the direct effect of the logistics strategy, organizational structure and logistics information technology (LIT) on organization performance of manufacturing firms in Negeri Sembilan, Malaysia. Findings revealed that all three variables were positively and significantly related to organizational performance.

This study has provided empirical contribution to the logistics system by integrating three independent variables on a dependent variable in a theoretical model underpinned by the resource-based view (RBV) theory. The findings proved that logistics strategy, organizational structure and logistics information technology play the important roles to the performance of manufacturing firms that can positively impact on economic growth and to develop the competitive advantages in the highly dynamic business environment.

REFERENCES

Adewale, G., Adesola, M., & Oyewale, I. (2013). Impact of marketing strategy on service performance: A study of selected small and medium enterprises (SME's) in Oluyole local government, Ibadan, Nigeria. *Journal of Business and Management*, 11(4), 59-66.

Agata, M.-L. (2015). Effects of IT use in improving customer service logistic processes. *Procedia Computer Science*, 65(2015), 961-970.

Aloulou, W. J. (2018). Impacts of strategic orientations on new product development and firm performance : Insights from Saudi industrial firm. *European Journal of Innovation Management*, 1(1), 1-18.

Angappa, G., Nachiappan, S., & Thanos, P. (2015). Information Technology for competitive advantage within logistics and supply chain : A Review. *Science Direct*, 99(1), 14-33.

Armstrong, J. S., & Overton, T. S. (1977). Estimating Non Response Bias Mail Surveys. *Journal of Marketing Research*, 14, 396-402.

Arthur, A., Stephen, O., Wilson, T., & Ronald, T. (2016). Information Technology capability, adoption, logistics service quality and the performance of third party logistics providers. *European Journal of Logistics, Purchasing and Supply Chain Management*, 4(2), 11-33.

Ayantoyinbo, B. B. (2015). Assessing the impact of information and communication technology (ICT) on the performance of freight distribution. *European Journal of Logistics, Purchasing and Supply Chain Management*, 3(4), 18-29.

Baiyi, W., & Fan, Y. (2011). The impact of internal logistics information technology processes to service performance. *Conference on Mechatronic Science, Electric Engineering and Computer (MEC)* (pp. 802-806). Jilin: IEEE Xplore.

Banerjee, S., & Srivastava, D. (2017). Organizational structure in Indian context. *International Journal of Civic Engagement and Social Change*, 4(2), 1-12.

Barney, J. (1991). Firm Resources and Sustained Competitive Advantage. *Journal of Management*, 99-120.

Barney, J. B. (2001). Resource-based theories of competitive advantage: A ten-year retrospective on the resource-based view. *Journal of management*, 1 (1-18).

Bartlett, M. (1954). A note on the multiplying factors for various chi square approximations. *Journal of the Royal Statistical Society*, Vol:16, 296-298.

Bawayarapu, H. B. (2005). *Knowledge management strategies and logistics firm performance.* Unpublished doctoral dissertation, University of Western Ontario, London, US.

Bhandari, R. (2014). Impact of technology on logistics and supply chain management. *IOSR Journal of Business and Management (IOSR-JBM)*, 1(1), 19-24.

Bohte, J., & Meier, K. J. (2001). Structure and the performance of public organizations: Task difficulty and span of control. *Public Organization Review*, 1, 341-354.

Borella, M. R., Barcellos, P. F., Sachdev, H., Russ, M. G., & Galelli, A. (2017). Organizational structure, service capability and its impact on business performance of logistics providers in the B2B context. *Margareth RoG&P Journal*, 24(2), 355-369.

Chua, Y. P. (2006). *Kaedah dan statistik penyelidikan: Kaedah penyelidikan*. Kuala Lumpur: McGraw-Hill Education.

Cohen, S., & Roussel, J. (2005). *Strategic Supply Chain Management : The Five Disciplines for Top Performance*. New York, NY.: McGraw-Hill.

Cortes, J. A., Serna, M. D., & Gomez, R. A. (2013). *Information systems applied to transport improvement*. Unpublished master thesis, University of Colombo, Colombo, Sri Lanka.

Creswell, J. W., & Creswell, J. D. (2018). *Research Design : Qualitative, Quantitative, and Mixed Methods Approaches*. Thousand Oaks: Sage Publications Inc.

Cronbach, L. J. (2004). My current thoughts on coefficient alpha and successor procedures. *Educational and Psychological Measurement*, 64, 391–418.

Dillman, D. A. (1999). *The design and administration of mail surveys*. Washington: Pullman.

Espino-Rodríguez, T. F., & Gil-Padilla, A. M. (2015). The structural and infrastructural decisions of operations management in the hotel sector and their impact on organizational performance. *Tourism and Hospitality Research*, 15(1), 3-18.

Evans, P. B., & Wurster, T. S. (1997). Evans, Phillip BStrategy and the New Economics of Information. *Harvard Business Review*, 75(5) 70-82.

Farhanghi, A. A., Abbaspour, A., & Ghassemi, R. A. (2013). The effect of Information Technology on organizational structure and firm performance: An analysis of

Consultant Engineers Firms (CEF) in Iran. *Procedia - Social and Behavioral Sciences*, 1(1), 644 – 649.

Gemeinhardt, G. (1997). *Unique characteristics of non-profit organizations: An investigation of their manifestation and impact on strategy and performance in non-profit and proprietary nursing homes.* Unpublished doctoral dissertation, University of Houston, Houston, USA.

Ghiani, G., Laporte, G., & Musmanno, R. (2013). *Introduction to logistics systems management.* New Jersey: John Wiley & Sons.

Gokus, O. (2008). *Configuration of market oriented culture, organizational structure and business strategy types and their performance implications in service organizations.* Ann Arbor: ProQuest LLC.

Green, J. K., Dwayne, W., Inman, & Anthony, R. (2008). The impact of logistics performance on organizational performance in a supply chain context. *Research paper*, 13(4), 317 –327.

Green, K. W., Whitten, G. D., & Inman, R. A. (2008). Supply Chain Management. *The Impact of Logistics Performance on Organizational Performance in a Supply*, 13(4), 317-327.

Gu, F. F., Hung, K., & Tse, D. K. (2008). When Does Guanxi Matter? Issues of Capitalization and Its Dark Sides. *Journal of Marketing*, 72(4), 12-28.

Hair, J. &., Babin, W. &., Anderson, B. &., & Rolph. (2009). *Hair, J & Black, W & Babin, Barry & Anderson, Rolph. (2009). Multivariate data analysis. Prentice Hall. London. .* London: Prentice Hall.

Hair, J., Anderson, R., Tatham, R., & Black, W. (1998). *Multivariate data analysis. 5th Edition.* New Jersey: Prentice Hall.

Handfield, R. B., & Bechtel, C. (2001). The role of trust and relationship structure in improving supply chain responsiveness. *Industrial Marketing Management*, 31 (2002) 367– 382.

Henry, M. (2016). *Exploring Information Technology: Why the use of Information Technology governance negatively influences revenue performance.* Unpublished doctoral dissertation, Capale University, Minneapolis, US.

Hosseini, S. S., Tekmedash, Y. N., Karami, A., & Jabarzadeh, Y. (2019). The impact of knowledge management strategy on service innovation performance in private and public hospitals. *Iranian Journal of Management Studies*, 12(1), 1-24.

Husso, M., & Nybakk, E. (2010). Importance of internal and external factors when adapting to environmental changes in SME sawmills in Norway and Finland: The manager's view. *Journal of forest products business research*, 7(1).

Islam, M., Hamid, A. A., & M.A.Karim. (2007). Manufacturing practices and performances: A Malaysian study. *International Review of Business Research papers*, 3(2),147-161.

Ittner, C. D., Larcker, D. F., & Randall, T. (2003). Service performance implications of strategic performance measurement in logistics services firms. *Accounting, organizations and society*, 28(7-8), 715-741.

Kachitvichyanukul, V., Sethanan, K., & Dawson, P. G. (2015). *Toward sustainable operations of supply chain and logistics systems (Eco-production).* Cham: Springer Publication.

Kaiser, H. F. (1974). An index of factorial simplicity. *Psychometrika*, vol:39, 31–36.

Kaur, C. R. (2004). Maritime Institute of Malaysia (MIMA). *International convention for the control and management of ships ballast water and sediments (BWM)* (pp. 18 - 44). Kuala Lumpur: Centre for Maritime Security and Environment (MSE).

Kawasaki, T., Hanaoka, S., & Le, H. T. (2010). *The impact of Information and Communication Technology on performance of logistics service providers in Vietnam.* Tokyo: JSCE Publications.

Khalid, K., Hilman, H., & Kuma, D. (2012). Get along with quantitative research process. *International Journal of Research in Management,* 2(2), 15-29.

Kim, Hwan, K., Günther, & Hans-Otto. (2007). *Container terminals and cargo systems : Design & Operations Management.* New York: Zpringer Publication.

Kimani, K. A. (2015). *Impact of information technology on organizational performance : Case of population services Kenya.* Unpublished master thesis, University of Nairobi, Nairobi, Kenya.

Knott, A. (1998). *Managed care strategies and the performance of rural hospitals.* Unpubished doctoral dissertation, University of Iowa, Ann Arbor, USA.

Kraaijenbrink, J., Spender, J., & Groen, A. J. (2010). The Resource-Based View: A review and assessment of Its critiques. *Journal of Management,* 36(1), 349-372.

Kyengo, M. F. (2014). *The relationship between manufacturing strategy and operational performance within the metal & allied sector in Kenya.* Unpublished doctoral dissertation, University of Nairobi, Nairobi, Kenya.

Mahmood, A. (2000). *Export specialization and competitiveness of the Malaysian manufacturing: Trends, challenges and prospects.* Melbourne.

McMillan, J. H., & Schumacher, S. (2001). *Research in education: A conceptual introduction (5th ed.).* New York: Longman.

Mollenkopf, Diane, Ozanne, & Lucie, A. G. (2000). The integration of marketing and logistics functions: An empirical examination o f New Zealand firms. *Journal of Business Logistics*, 21 (2), 89-112.

Morrison, K., Manion, L., & Cohen, L. (2011). *Research Methods in Education*. New York: Routledge.

Nchorbuno, D. A., Shafiwu, A. B., & Ayamga, B. N. (2017). The impact of organisational structures on services to Polytechnic students. *Asian Journal of Economics*, 5(2), 1-13.

Niu, Y. (2010). *The impact of Information Technology on Supply Chain performance*. Unpublished doctoral dissertation, University of North Carolina, Charlotte, US.

Nwonu, C. O., Dr. Agbaeze, E. K., & Obi-Anike, H. O. (2017). Effect of organisational structure on performance of selected manufacturing companies in Enugu State, Nigeria. *The International Journal Of Business and Management*, 5(5), 190-206.

Olah, J., Karmazin, G., Peto, K., & Popp, J. (2017). Information technology developments of logistics service providers in Hungary. *International Journal of Logistics Research and Applications*, 1(1), 332-344.

Osayuwamen, O. (2018). Influence of Information Technology and Logistics integration and delivery reliability of small and medium enterprises in Gauteng province (China). *International Journal of eBusiness and eGovernment studies*, 10(1), 34-50.

Pallant, J. (2007). *SPSS Survival Manual: A Step by Step Guide to Data Analysis Using SPSS for Windows*. 3rd Edition. New York: McGraw Hill Open University Press.

Ratna, R., & Kaur, T. (2016). The impact of Information Technology on job related factors like health and safety, job satisfaction, performance, productivity and work life balance. *Journal of Business & Financial Affairs*, 5(1), 1-9.

Rehman, M. A. (2017). *How multiple strategic orientation affect the service performance of B2B SME's*. Unpublished doctoral dissertation, University of Oulu, Oulu, Finland.

Richards, G. (2014). *Warehouse Management: A complete guide to improving efficiency and minimizing costs in the modern warehouse (Second Edition)*. Londan: Kogan Page Limited.

Roberts, J. G. (2015). *IT adoption within veteran service organization and non-profit organizations: A descriptive study*. Unpublished doctoral dissertation, University of Phoenix, Phoenix, US.

Saunders, M., Lewis, P., & Thornhill, A. (2012). *Research Methods for Business Students*. Harlow: Pearson Education Ltd.

Schellenberg, D. S. (2013). *Issues in strategy implementation: The effect of congruence among strategy, structure and managerial performance criteria on service performance*. Unpublished doctoral dissertation, Indiana University, Bloomington, USA.

Sekaran, U. (2003). *Research methods for business*. New York: John Wiley & Sons Inc.

Shaharudin, M. R., Rashid, N. R., Wangbenmad, C., Hotrawaisaya, C., & Wararatcha, P. (2018). A content analysis of current issues in Supply Chain Management. *Research Gate*, 7(5), 199-212.

Smith, J. S. (2007). *An examination of the relationship between service recovery system structure, service operating environment and recovery performance*. Unpublished doctoral dissertation, University of South Carolina, Columbia, US.

Smith, T. M., & Reece, J. S. (1998). The relationship of strategy, fit, productivity and business performance in a services setting. *Journal of Operations Management*, 17(9), 145–161.

Sosiawani, I., Ramli, A. B., Mustafa, M. B., & Yusoff, R. Z. (2015). Strategic planning and firm performance : A proposed framework. *International Academic research Journal of Business and Technology*, 1(2), 201-207.

Szymonik, A. (2012). *Logistics and Supply Chain Management*. New York: Research Gate.

Tabachnick, B. G., & Fidell, L. S. (2007). *Using Multivariate Statistics (5th ed.)*. New York: Allyn and Bacon.

Tan, R. H., Ng, Y. J., Fong, S. T., Chong, S. Y., & Sukumaran, V. (2016). Factors Affecting the Business Performance of Small and Medium Enterprises (SMEs) For Tourism Industry in Malaysia: Evidence from Penang. *Final Year Project, UTAR*.

Tang, Wong, W. P., & Foon, C. (2018). The major determinants of logistic performance in a global perspective: evidence from panel data analysis. *International Journal of Logistics Research and Applications*, 1(1), 431-443.

Tavitiyaman, P., Zhang, H. Q., & Qu, H. (2012). The effect of competitive strategies and organizational structure on hotel performance. *International Journal of Contemporary Hospitality Management*, 24(1), 140-159.

Tilanus, B. (1997). *Information Systems in Logistics and Transportation*. Somerville, MA : Emerald Group Publishing Limited.

Toriello, J. A. (2017). *The effects of organizational structure on supplier performance in purchasing: A quantitative predictive study*. Unpublished doctoral dissertation, Capella University, Minneapolis, US.

Tracey, M. (1998). The importance of logistics efficiency of customer service and firm performance. *The international Journal of Logistics Management,*, 9(2), 65-81.

Troyer, L. (1995). *Team Embeddedness : The relations between team social structures, organization social structures and team performance.* Unpublished doctoral dissertation, Stanford University, Stanford, US.

Wilson, M. N., Iravo, D. M., Tirimba, O. I., & Ombui, D. (2015). Effects of Information Technology on performance of logistics firms in Nairobi County. *International Journal of Scientific and Research Publications,* 5(4), 1-26.

Wu, Y. C. (2018). *The effects of strategic change on innovative performance in Taiwanese SME's: The impacts of CEO's personality, top management team behaviour and organizational culture.* Unpublished doctoral dessertation, Alliant International University, San Diego, California.

Yavuz, M., & Deligonul, B. (2017). The importance of logistics Information Technologies and knowledge management capabilities on intermediaries performance. *ResearchGate,* 1(1), 208-224.

Yusuf, Y. Y., Gunasekaran, A., Adeleye, E. O., & Sivayoganathan, K. (2004). Agile supply chain capabilities : Determinants of competitive objectives. *European Journal of Operational Research, Elsevier,* vol. 159(2), 379-392.

Zakaria, H., Zailani, S., & Fernando, Y. (2010). Moderating role of logistics Information Technology on the logistics relationships and logistics service quality. *Operations & Supply Chain Management,* 3(3), 134-147.

Zakariah, Z. M., Hooi, T. K., & Ahmad, A. R. (2004). *UNEP/GEF SCS Project National Corals and Coral Reef Report Malaysia.* Kuala Lumpur: MIMA.

Zolla, R. W. (1988). *Environment, strategy and performance in the professional service firm.* Unpublished doctoral dissertation, University of Houston, Massachusetts, USA.

APPENDICES

APPENDIX 1

Questionaire

SURVEY QUESTIONNAIRE

Dear Respondents,

You are hereby invited to participate in a survey to examine the effect of logistics strategy, organizational structure and logistics information technology process on organization performance in manufacturing firms. Participation in this survey is completely voluntary. If you agree to participate, please complete the questionnaire attached. There is no right or wrong answer in this questionnaire. All information provided will be stored confidentially.

NOTE:

Please complete this questionnaire by selecting the best response by indicate how you agree or disagree with each statement that describe the degree of logistics strategies, organizational structure, logistics information technology processes and the organization performance in your company. It is important to answer all questions.

Thank you for your time and cooperation.

Yours faithfully,

Archanaa Kappan
PBS MBA Student
PUTRA Business School
University Putra Malaysia
HP: 010-2130067
Email: archanaa7327@gmail.com

SECTION A: DEMOGRAPHY

Please thick (√) in an appropriate box and indicate correct answer at item 7 and 8.

1.	Gender	Male	
		Female	
2.	Ethnicity	Malay	
		Chinese	
		Indian	
		Others: ………………………	
3.	Age (Years)	25 and below	
		26 – 30	
		31 – 40	
		41 – 50	
		Above 51	
4.	Education Level	Diploma	
		Bachelor Degree	

		Master Degree
		PhD
5.	Job Position	Volunteer
		Non-executive / Operational
		Snr. Executive / Middle Management
		Snr Management / Managers
		Top Management
6.	Experience in present Organization (years)	Less than 1
		1 - 3
		4 - 6
		7 – 9
		More than 10

7. Nature of business ....
8. Annual gross sales (MYR) ....

INSTRUCTIONS:

Please complete this questionnaire by selecting the best response by placing a circle in the appropriate answer. It is important to answer all questions.

Strongly Agree	5
Agree	4
Neutral	3
Disagree	2
Strongly Disagree	1

SECTION B: LOGISTICS STRATEGY

These are statements that describe the degree of logistics strategies and practices in your organization. Please indicate how you agree or disagree with each statement based on the scales below. Make a circle on any scale that you feel appropriate.

No.	Item					
1.	Primary objective of logistics is to effectively manage activities that results in supply chain, manufacturing and distribution costs	5	4	3	2	1
2.	Logistics functions are managed as a value-added system	5	4	3	2	1
3.	Logistics facilitates the management of information flows among channel members (manufacturer, distributors, wholesalers, dealers, retailers and customers)	5	4	3	2	1
4.	Logistics facilitates the coordination of several business units in order to provide competitive customer service	5	4	3	2	1
5.	Logistics facilitates inter-organizational coordination through cooperation and collaboration with dealers or distributors	5	4	3	2	1

SECTION C: ORGANIZATIONAL STRUCTURE

These are statements that describe the degree of centralization or decentralization in your organization that used in making the following decision. Please indicate how you agree or disagree with each statement based on the scales below. Make a tick circle on any scale that you feel appropriate.

No.	Item					
1.	Less traditional structures are more loosely woven and flexible with the ability to respond quickly to changing business environments	5	4	3	2	1
2.	Achieving alignment and sustaining organizational capacity requires time and critical thinking	5	4	3	2	1
3.	Strategy must continually drive organization structure and people decisions, and the structure and design must reflect and enable effective leadership	5	4	3	2	1
4.	Five elements will create an effective organizational structure: job design, departmentalization, delegation (empowerment), span of control and chain of command	5	4	3	2	1
5.	Organizational realignment involves closing the structural gaps and power distance that impeding organizational performance	5	4	3	2	1

SECTION D: LOGISTICS INFORMATION TECHNOLOGY (LIT)

These are statements that describe the degree of logistics information technology processes and practices in your organization. Please indicate how you agree or disagree with each statement based on the scales below. Make a circle on any scale that you feel appropriate.

No.	Item					
1.	Integrating new technology into existing logistic operations can help in increasing customer service, reduce cost and streamline supply chains	5	4	3	2	1
2.	Logistics information systems promote the flexible use and coordination of resources to support knowledge management skills and quick decision making	5	4	3	2	1
3.	Firm and industry have increased the use of Electronic Data Interchange (EDI) standards, integrated inventory system, transportation and warehousing planning system during the past three years	5	4	3	2	1
4.	Logistics information technology (LIT) provide real-time tracking and accurate delivery systems	5	4	3	2	1
5.	The emerging new technologies are creating strategic opportunities for the organizations to build competitive advantages in various functional areas of management	5	4	3	2	1

SECTION E: ORGANIZATION PERFORMANCE

These are statements that describe the perceptual measurement of firm performance using combination of financial, marketing and less traditional measurement on service performance in your organization. Please indicate how you agree or disagree with each statement based on the scales below. Make a circle on any scale that you feel appropriate.

No.	Item					
1.	Organization has the ability to meet quoted or anticipated delivery dates on a consistent basis	5	4	3	2	1
2.	Accommodate delivery times, handle difficulties, non-standard orders and handle product modifications upon customer request	5	4	3	2	1
3.	Perform value added services for customers during the warehouse or distribution processes	5	4	3	2	1
4.	Attain the lowest total supply chain cost by achieving high volume output (economy of scale)	5	4	3	2	1
5.	Perceived logistics performance matches with customer expectations and company goals	5	4	3	2	1

APPENDIX 2

SPSS RESULTS

Reliability

Notes		
Output Created		18-JUL-2019 02:44:42
Comments		
Input	Data	C:\Users\archaana\Documents\projectpaper
	Active Dataset	DataSet1
	Filter	<none>
	Weight	<none>
	Split File	<none>
	N of Rows in Working Data File	136
	Matrix Input	C:\Users\archaana\Documents\project paper

Missing Value Handling	Definition of Missing	User-defined missing values are treated as missing.
	Cases Used	Statistics are based on all cases with valid data for all variables in the procedure.
Syntax		reliability/variables= q1 q2 q3 q4 q5 q6 q7 q8 q9 q10 q11 q12 q13 q14 q15 q16 q17 q18 q19 q20/scale ('book 1') all/model=alpha/statistic=descriptive scale corr/summary=total.
Resources	Processor Time	00:00:00.08
	Elapsed Time	00:00:00.08

Case Processing Summary		N	%
Cases	Valid	136	100.0
	Excluded [a]	0	.0
	Total	136	100.0

Item Statistics (Page 1/2)	Mean	Std. Deviation	N
Organization has the ability to meet quoted or anticipated delivery dates on a consistent basis	3.81	.661	136
Accommodate delivery times, handle difficulties, non-standard orders and handle product modifications upon customer request	3.79	.671	136
Perform value added services for customers during the warehouse or distribution processes	3.81	.830	136
Attain the lowest total supply chain cost by achieving high volume output (economy of scale)	3.84	.809	136

	Mean	Std. Deviation	N
Perceived logistics performance matches with customer expectations and company goals	3.91	.745	136
Primary objective of logistics is to effectively manage activities that results in supply chain, manufacturing and distribution costs	3.99	.873	136
Logistics functions are managed as a value-added system	3.90	.846	136
Logistics facilitates the management of information flows among channel members (manufacturer, distributors, wholesalers, dealers, retailers and customers)	3.95	.792	136
Logistics facilitates the coordination of several business units in order to provide competitive customer service	3.84	.680	136
Logistics facilitates the coordination of several business units in order to provide competitive customer service	3.84	.680	136
Logistics facilitates the coordination of several business units in order to provide competitive customer service	3.84	.680	136
Logistics facilitates the coordination of several business units in order to provide competitive customer service	3.84	.680	136
Logistics facilitates the coordination of several business units in order to provide competitive customer service	3.84	.680	136

Item Statistics (Page 2/2)	Mean	Std. Deviation	N
Logistics facilitates the coordination of several business units in order to provide competitive customer service	3.84	.680	136
Logistics facilitates the coordination of several business units in order to provide competitive customer service	3.84	.680	136

Statement	Mean	SD	N
Logistics facilitates inter-organizational coordination through cooperation and collaboration with dealers or distributors	3.79	.668	136
Less traditional structures are more loosely woven and flexible with the ability to respond quickly to changing business environments	3.68	.708	136
Achieving alignment and sustaining organizational capacity requires time and critical thinking	3.88	.861	136
Strategy must continually drive organization structure and people decisions, and the structure and design must reflect and enable effective leadership	3.94	.697	136
Five elements will create an effective organizational structure: job design, departmentalization, delegation (empowerment), span of control and chain of command	3.89	.892	136
Organizational realignment involves closing the structural gaps and power distance that impeding organizational performance	3.70	.846	136
Integrating new technology into existing logistic operations can help in increasing customer service, reduce cost and streamline supply chains	4.06	.777	136
Logistics information systems promote the flexible use and coordination of resources to support knowledge management skills and quick decision making	3.89	.727	136
Firm and industry have increased the use of Electronic Data Interchange (EDI) standards, integrated inventory system, transportation and warehousing planning system during the past three years	3.63	.850	136

Logistics information technology (LIT) provide real-time tracking and accurate delivery systems	3.91	.774	136
The emerging new technologies are creating strategic opportunities for the organizations to build competitive advantages in various functional areas of management	4.08	.700	136

Item-Total Statistics

Item-Total Statistics					
Questionnaire Items	Scale Mean if Item Deleted	Scale Variance if Item Deleted	Corrected Item-Total Correlation	Squared Multiple Correlation	Cronbach's Alpha if Item Deleted
Q1	73.48	192.785	.912	.	.992
Q2	73.50	192.652	.905	.	.992
Q3	73.48	187.525	.957	.	.992
Q4	73.45	188.323	.945	.	.992
Q5	73.37	189.703	.960	.	.992
Q6	73.29	187.246	.919	.	.992
Q7	73.39	187.025	.961	.	.992
Q8	73.34	188.937	.937	.	.992
Q9	73.45	191.908	.934	.	.992
Q10	73.49	192.400	.924	.	.992
Q11	73.61	191.914	.894	.	.992
Q12	73.40	186.717	.956	.	.992
Q13	73.35	191.546	.930	.	.992
Q14	73.40	186.019	.952	.	.992
Q15	73.59	187.933	.919	.	.992
Q16	73.23	189.629	.922	.	.992
Q17	73.40	190.286	.955	.	.992
Q18	73.65	187.961	.913	.	.992
Q19	73.37	188.814	.966	.	.992

| Q20 | 73.21 | 192.105 | .896 | . | .992 |

Scale Statistics			
Mean	Variance	Std. Deviation	N of Items
77.29	209.969	14.490	20

Reliability Statistics		
Cronbach's Alpha	Cronbach's Alpha Based on Standardized Items	N of Items
.993	.993	20

Inter-Item Correlation Matrix

	Q1	Q2	Q3	Q4	Q5	Q6	Q7	Q8	Q9	Q10	Q11	Q12	Q13	Q14	Q15	Q16	Q17	Q18	Q19	Q20
Q1	1	0.976	0.891	0.869	0.868	0.754	0.865	0.802	0.919	0.916	0.879	0.884	0.828	0.831	0.85	0.786	0.88	0.888	0.878	0.786
Q2	0.976	1	0.91	0.891	0.851	0.743	0.848	0.788	0.898	0.893	0.898	0.866	0.813	0.814	0.864	0.777	0.862	0.9	0.861	0.778
Q3	0.891	0.91	1	0.946	0.931	0.856	0.942	0.909	0.863	0.864	0.864	0.953	0.877	0.912	0.898	0.856	0.91	0.897	0.93	0.843
Q4	0.869	0.891	0.946	1	0.91	0.847	0.917	0.877	0.84	0.842	0.89	0.929	0.85	0.909	0.902	0.863	0.888	0.882	0.946	0.847
Q5	0.868	0.851	0.931	0.91	1	0.887	0.926	0.921	0.936	0.901	0.83	0.907	0.932	0.922	0.862	0.892	0.98	0.849	0.962	0.866
Q6	0.754	0.743	0.856	0.847	0.887	1	0.901	0.931	0.846	0.823	0.774	0.895	0.9	0.94	0.859	0.95	0.874	0.804	0.886	0.91
Q7	0.865	0.848	0.942	0.917	0.926	0.901	1	0.932	0.872	0.88	0.822	0.98	0.87	0.967	0.857	0.9	0.909	0.864	0.959	0.89
Q8	0.802	0.788	0.909	0.877	0.921	0.931	0.932	1	0.865	0.834	0.776	0.914	0.934	0.905	0.828	0.92	0.904	0.841	0.923	0.903
Q9	0.919	0.898	0.863	0.84	0.936	0.846	0.872	0.865	1	0.953	0.859	0.853	0.902	0.874	0.867	0.845	0.952	0.87	0.901	0.806
Q10	0.916	0.893	0.864	0.842	0.901	0.823	0.88	0.834	0.953	1	0.891	0.859	0.865	0.882	0.859	0.823	0.914	0.857	0.91	0.781
Q11	0.879	0.898	0.864	0.89	0.83	0.774	0.822	0.776	0.859	0.891	1	0.836	0.802	0.822	0.924	0.788	0.836	0.932	0.839	0.755
Q12	0.884	0.866	0.953	0.929	0.907	0.895	0.98	0.914	0.853	0.859	0.836	1	0.853	0.948	0.866	0.896	0.89	0.871	0.94	0.889
Q13	0.828	0.813	0.877	0.85	0.932	0.9	0.87	0.934	0.902	0.865	0.802	0.853	1	0.872	0.849	0.909	0.952	0.838	0.897	0.876
Q14	0.831	0.814	0.912	0.909	0.922	0.94	0.967	0.905	0.874	0.882	0.822	0.948	0.872	1	0.898	0.897	0.907	0.835	0.951	0.857
Q15	0.85	0.864	0.898	0.902	0.862	0.859	0.857	0.828	0.867	0.859	0.924	0.866	0.849	0.898	1	0.816	0.873	0.916	0.864	0.767
Q16	0.786	0.777	0.856	0.863	0.892	0.95	0.9	0.92	0.845	0.823	0.788	0.896	0.909	0.897	0.816	1	0.877	0.818	0.895	0.945
Q17	0.88	0.862	0.91	0.888	0.98	0.874	0.909	0.904	0.952	0.914	0.836	0.89	0.952	0.907	0.873	0.877	1	0.857	0.943	0.848
Q18	0.888	0.9	0.897	0.882	0.849	0.804	0.864	0.841	0.87	0.857	0.932	0.871	0.838	0.835	0.916	0.818	0.857	1	0.85	0.772
Q19	0.878	0.861	0.93	0.946	0.962	0.886	0.959	0.923	0.901	0.91	0.839	0.94	0.897	0.951	0.864	0.895	0.943	0.85	1	0.875
Q20	0.786	0.778	0.843	0.847	0.866	0.91	0.89	0.903	0.806	0.781	0.755	0.889	0.876	0.857	0.767	0.945	0.848	0.772	0.875	1

THE RELATIONSHIP OF CORPORATE SOCIAL RESPONSIBILITY ON PURCHASE INTENTIONS OF GENERATION Y IN MALAYSIA

CHAPTER 1

Foreword

Overview

The concept of corporate social responsibility (CSR) has come to the spotlight about 65 years ago where G. Bowen first published the book "Social responsibilities of the businessman" on year 1953 (Smith, 2011). He defined CSR as "the obligations of business to pursue those policies, to make those decisions or to follow those lines of action which are desirable in terms of the objectives and values of our society (Bowen, 1953)." Since then, many studies were done to specify the concept and content of social responsibility. It has redefined as the company's voluntary responsibilities on different aspects, which are economic, legal, ethical and philanthropic towards the society it serves (Carroll, 1979; 1991). Eventually, CSR has become popular amongst the academics, employers, researchers, communities and the government from all over the world (Mamun, Shaikh & Easmin, 2017).

Particularly, CSR has been growing popularity in Malaysia (Hopkins, 2003; Nasir, Halim, Sallem, Jasni & Aziz, 2015). Currently, CSR is an emerging trend in business to address the social and environmental impact through the company activities. As CSR is related to the human rights, social issues and environmental impact, thus the corporations have recognized the importance of CSR (Sharma & Mehta, 2012). Besides that, it is also emphasized the importance of CSR through the engagement of leadership in CSR activities, respond and integrate with the interests of the stakeholders in the global companies (Keegan & Green, 2013).

Besides that, the society has expected the company to form a "social contract" where it is rooted on the values and expectations of what a company should do in order to preserve its orders. Therefore, it is also of the best interest of the company to adhere to this agreement. Hence, participation in the CSR activities will serve as one of the determinants on the sustainability of the company (Deegan & Unerman, 2011). Moreover, the companies engaged in the CSR activities also related to the improvement of the financial performance, increase in the customers' reputation as well as attract talented employees to join the companies (Tsoutsoura, 2004; Margolis, Elfenbein & Walsh, 2007). CSR also act as the proponent in buying intention and built of reputation for the growth of the firms as such that the failing in reputation will be severe for the future profits (Margolis et al, 2007). According to Mohr, Webb and Harris (2001), the firms are under the political scrutiny and pressure in order to behave in a socially responsible way. One of the requirements for public-listed companies in Malaysia is the mandate to disclosure the financial records as well as the introduction of CSR dimensions in one of the Bursa Malaysia's guidelines (Darus, 2012). The perception is to ensure the firms could be a good citizen to provide solutions to the communities' issues in a socially acceptable manner, as well as to take care of the environmental and aid in the charities.

Since consumers are getting more concern of the origins of what they consume, their environmental footprint, and increased awareness to social and moral queues, many businesses has adopted CSR as an essential component be it in the way materials are source, the manufacturing processes, waste management or the timely payment of taxes (Sharma, 2015). Malaysians are getting concern over the corporate social responsibility with the media influence and better education. With increasing education level, more and more consumers are aware for the need of CSR (Rahim, Jalaludin & Tajuddin, 2011). Particularly, the generation Y have been joining the middle age with increasing purchasing power, thus, it is important for the companies to understand the expectations of this generation to trigger their purchase intention. With the increasing awareness of generation Y on environment and social issues, their attitudes towards the companies' CSR are important aspects of their purchase intention (Hwang, Lee & Diddi, 2013; Ekström, Hjelmgren & Salomonson, 2015). They are value-seeking and had been grown up with the well-verse of technology that willing to engage with the companies to let them know what they want and demand for (Black, 2010). Therefore, the consumer behaviour of generation Y is not only focus on the products and service but also on the response of the corporations towards society and environmental.

With the increasing population of generation Y in Malaysia as well as the increasing purchasing power of this newly joined workforce, it is important to understand their market needs and expectation. Research conducted by Hwang et al (2013) has indicated that generation Y has increasing aware about the environmental and social issues a such that one of the key aspects of their purchase intention is the CSR of the corporation.

Therefore, it is a need to investigate on the effect of CSR on the purchase intention of Malaysian generation Y and how it effects on their purchase intention.

Problem Diagnosed

According to research done by Crowther (2003) and Mohr and Webb (2005), the corporations will receive the positive effect if the corporations embrace CSR. Parsa, Lord, Putrevu & Kreeger (2015) has demonstrated that the positive effects of consumers towards companies that involved in CSR activities. Lee and Lee (2015) has further justified that contribution of CSR activities towards the image of the companies, the purchase intention of the consumers as well as the firm's long-term finance performance (Ko, Taylor, Wagner & Ji, 2008; Lee, Han, Hsu & Kim., 2010). Besides that, consumers also reward the companies through transactional reward and relational reward whereby, transactional reward imply on the willingness on purchase intention while relational reward is the built of brand loyalty (Du, Bhattacharya & Sen, 2007). Therefore, the customers will be more likely to be loyal and committed to the firms that operate in a socially responsible manner and take care of the environmental issues (Brown & Dacin, 1997; Pirsch, Gupta, & Grau, 2007). It is also mentioned that there is a positive association between consumers' awareness and purchase intention (Lee & Shin, 2010).

However, some research also has reported the findings are inconclusive and identified that the purchase intention and buying decisions of consumers are more focus on self-benefit rather than the interest on CSR activities and do not related to company performance (Sen & Bhattacharya, 2001; Vaaland, Heide, & Grønhaug, 2008; Fatma & Rahman, 2016). The experts comprised of leaders from Malaysia reputable cooperation also think that the perception towards CSR is just another fancy management concept and the PR approach to trigger the purchase intention in Malaysia (Lu & Castka, 2008). There are previous research shows that for those consumers who is not aware about the CSR programs conducted by the companies, would not have the effect on their purchase intention (Belk, Devinney & Eckhard, 2005; Sen, Bhattacharya & Korschun, 2006).

In contrary, when the consumer has showed supports towards the CSR activities, and then firm could use CSR as one of its factors in buying behaviours (Bhattacharya & Sen, 2004). Next, those consumers that have a higher education level are more aware and interest on CSR activities, which emphasis that they are willing to know more about the social issues and behaviours of the firms. Thus, they are also showing a higher willingness to pay more for the CSR products and willing to switch brands or stores (Mohr et al. 2001). Moreover, studies also indicated that consumers are able to categorize the type of CSR activities at which such activities are contribute to the society. As such, the impact of CSR activities contribute to society is higher than the one of environmental contributions (Öberseder, Schlegelmilch & Murphy, 2013; Lee & Shin, 2010). According to Beckmann (2007), the result showed that consumers are not willing to pay more for socially responsible products, but contrary to the research conducted by Mohr & Webb (2005) and Bhattacharya & Sen (2004), stated that consumers are willing to pay for the higher price on CSR products. When the CSR products are able to relate to the consumers' personal beliefs and values, then, the consumers are willing to pay a higher price for such products.

As different studies made on this topic, with partly contradict each other, thus, it is complex to study the influence of CSR on consumers (Lee & Shin, 2010). Former studies also demonstrated the differences of perception on CSR in each generation. Particularly, generation Y has been defined by McCrindle (2008) as the generation with higher educated, materially endowed as well as entertained and entrepreneurial. Hence, the impact of CSR activities might have an influence on Generation Y.

As of July 2018, there are about 7.4 billion people in the world while generation Y (those who born from 1981 to 1997) is accounts for 27% of the global population, equivalent to 2 billion people. They are in their young adulthood and would becoming the world's most vital generational cohort in the segment of consumer spending growth, sources of employees, and overall economic prospects. With significant impact to the business, it is important to understand this cohort. They are also being labelled as the high spending with strong power group (Farris, Chong & Dunning. 2002). Even though most of the Millennials are just students or just graduates, they are still having the highest disposable incomes compared to those youths in the history of the same ages (Foscht et al., 2009; Morton 2002). Former studies also categorize Generation Y as the larger consumer groups (Sullivan & Heitmeyer, 2008). Millennials are growing up in a globalization era with the advancement of technology and diverse demographic and cultural (Ng, Schweitzer & Lyons, 2009). Hence, they are more sensitive to information and thus also aware to the issues happening around them as such these alerts them to be concerned on social issues and wanting to contribute to the society (Paco, Alves, Shiel & Filho., 2013; Ng et al., 2009). According to Autio and Wilska (2005), millennials are on the front line for social issues and ethical consumption, which made them an interesting demographic group to study for CSR (Djamasbi et al., 2008).

As the generation Y is the rapid growing group of consumers with increasing purchasing power in the society (Smith, 2012), thus it is vital to determine the significant relationship of CSR on the purchase intention among Generation Y in Malaysia. Nevertheless, these studies are barely done on general perception of generation Y on the relationship between CSR and their purchase intention. Moreover, the CSR research are mostly done in European countries and America (Maignan, 2001) as the awareness on CSR activities has been conducted in given framework (Mohr et al., 2001). Besides that, it is also interesting to find that there is study done by Nasir et al. (2014), reported that the lack of awareness and perception on CSR in Malaysia. Moreover, former studies showed that consumer are lack of awareness towards companies' CSR activities, however, those consumers with a higher education would be more interested on the CSR activities and will be influenced on their purchase intension (Geokhaji, 2015).

Therefore, this study is to examine the former research that conducted on this subject matter and its variables, which have an impact on purchase intentions among Generation Y in Malaysia, such as the consumers' awareness of CSR, consumers' trust in CSR and the willingness to pay premium price.

Objectives

In general, the objective of this research is to determine the relationship between consumers' awareness of CSR, consumers' trust in CSR and willingness to pay a premium price and purchase intention among the generation Y in Malaysia.

Specifically, the objectives of study are:

1. To investigate the relationship between consumers' awareness of CSR and purchase intention among the generation Y in Malaysia.
2. To examine the relationship between consumers' trust in CSR and purchase intention among the generation Y in Malaysia.
3. To investigate the relationship between the willingness to pay a premium price and purchase intention among the generation Y in Malaysia.

This study focused on the current awareness of the generation Y aged from year 1983 to 2003 in Malaysia on CSR activities and its impact on the consumers' purchase intentions. This study is conducted quantitatively through online survey- questionnaire methods through social media by distributing to 500 target respondents. The data are analysed using multiple regression method to determine the strength of the relationships between each variable.

This research is to investigate the relationship between purchase intentions among Generation Y in Malaysia, with the CSR awareness, trust of CSR activities and the willingness to pay premium price. This research will provide the current view of generation Y in Malaysia towards CSR activities which help in marketing strategies and communication activities to increase the purchase intention of consumers. Besides that, this study provides a wider viewpoint from the generation Y on corporate social responsibility in Asian countries that able to allow the business to understand more about the purchase intention of consumers and provide the insights in giving the right type of marketing information, using the most influential marketing mediums as well as raise the consumer brand perception and brand loyalty.

CHAPTER 2

Desk Reviews

Generation Y

Generation Y is defined as the demographic cohort that born between years of 1979 and 1994 (Brosdahl and Carpenter, 2011). Different studies had defined Millennials differently, at which Alch, 2000 and Paul, 2001 has defined that those who is born on 1977 should be considered as millennials, while Neuborne & Kerwin, 1999 has considered only from 1979, while Howe & Strauss, 2000 is only take into consideration for those who born after 1982. As the ongoing timeframe, the ages of millennials have shifted. Hence, this study is taking into consideration for those who is born between 1983 and 2003 as Millennials. This is also allowing us to easily capture the total number of people as of 2018 according to the statistics reported by Department of Statistic Malaysia.

In Malaysia, there are total 32million of people as of 2018 as reported by Department of Statistic Malaysia. Between, there are about 12million of Generation Y aged between

15 and 35 (Table 2.1). This population are comprised of 23% of secondary school students aged from 15 to 19 who are teenagers who seeking for freedom in making their own purchase options, and thus will have specific wants and needs as a consumer. Whilst the 53% of young adult aged from 20 to 29 who are beginning to join the university and prepare to join the workforce. The balance of the 23% are aged from 30 to 34 who has been enter their middle age and having a higher purchasing power.

Table 2.1 The Malaysian Population by Age, 2018.

Age	Malaysian Population ('000)
0-4	2,595.6
5-9	2,559.6
10-14	2,549.6
15-19	2,871.1
20-24	3,232.1
25-29	3,281.3
30-34	2,868.5
35-39	2,438.4
40-44	1,950.9
45-49	1,768.9
50-54	1,619.8
55-59	1,418.5
60-64	1,131.5
65-69	843.5
70-74	573.1
75-79	338
80-84	197.5
85+	146.8

| Total | 32,384.7 |

Source: Department of Statistics, Malaysia, 2018

Generation Y is racially and ethnically diverse, more culturally liberal, and well versed in technology (Talbott, 2012). According to Alch (2000), this generation will be the focus group in the twenty-first century as research done by Paul (2001) has indicated that the consumer spending category in almost all the business has been eyeing on this generation because Farris, Chong and Dunning (2002) has agreed on this viewpoint that business that failed to pay attention to this group will be the biggest mistake.

Nevertheless, the focus group are mostly conducted in European countries and US (Syrett & Lammimam, 2004), as such the size of Millennial market and its impact will be differing from Asian countries like Malaysia. In 2018 there were 32million Millennials in Malaysia, about 13millions of which are generation Y (Statistics Malaysia, 2018) which represents quite a big market relatively to country's overall population, which is about 40% (Table 2.1).

Generation Y is differentiated from other generational cohorts due to its strong exposure to the Internet since young. They are more alerted to the information received and able to compare and value not only the brand but also the functional aspects. This means the Generation Y prefer good brand with good value and quality product (Geraci & Nagy, 2004). This is also supported by the research of Heaney and Gleeson (2008) whereby they defined generation Y is the 'most savvy and informed consumers who seeking for bargains by well-researched for online shopping transactions.

In the aspect of CSR, generation Y are having a higher trust on large national corporation than their parents as they believe these corporation will do good for them and the nation. In return, they are playing an important to these firms due to such expectation. They are more aware on the personal choices and actions compared to other generations (Howe & Strauss, 2000). Thus, Neuborne & Kerwin (1999) supported that this generation will made the dynamic changes in the corporate social policy.

Besides that, generation Y is more proficient in social policy making compared to former generations. Even for those who are not active in this social awareness also could exercise their rights as the consumers and workers towards the social irresponsible companies. This is further supported by the studied conducted by Sobczak, Debucquet & Havard (2006) on the assumption that young generations are more open to social and environmental issues. Subsequently, studies done by Alch (2000) and Ng, Schwitzer & Lyons (2010) has indicated that generation Y are concern about global issues in general and have a high tendency to "save the world", which resulting this generation to be more aware and having a higher expectation to firms on their social responsibility and the ethical behaviour.

In a nationwide survey of Millennial behaviours and motivations, over 75% of respondents reported good citizenship as being a trait which is highly important to them and influential in decision making ("How the new generation of Millennials will change travel and tourism", 2011). Therefore, as this generation values moral behaviours and considers themselves to be socially responsible citizens, as socially responsible consumers, generation Y will seek out products from companies who strive to help society (Mohr, Webb, & Harris, 2001). Generation Y have the tendency to be format agnostic, which see only little credibility differences between print and media formats, as well as demand for information and entertainment easily access at anytime and anywhere (Abram & Luther, 2004).

According to Alch (2000), the properties of generation Y tends to be in command on their environment in order to receive information faster and easier, and have more personal time with less-structured lifestyles. In additional to that, generation Y also behave to be more loyal to their close reference group and highly valued on the information given by their peers but very defensive towards the selling information given by third party or sellers (Syrett & Lammimam, 2004).

This is further supported by Geraci & Nagy (2004), Abram & Luther (2004) and McCasland (2005) which stated that the generation Y lives in transition surrounded by fragmented media through various media. Hence, it is challenging to reach to these young consumers. They are also good for their multitasking, because they are being exposed to multiple commercial messages since young age. Therefore, they are able to differentiate and cope with the persuasion attempts from the organization (Friestad & Wright, 1994). Moreover, studies from Neubrone & Kerwin (1999) has supported that this generation also respond differently from their parents due to the growing up circumstances with full of media and brands. Hence, the marketers have to instil their message to the core of this generation, into their reference group in order to disseminate the information to this group. However, they do not hate advertising, just that they do not prefer irrelevant and unwanted advertising (McCasland, 2005). Hence, getting to know the preference of generation Y would be able to tackle their interest and customize the marketing strategies to connect with generation Y (Neuborne & Kerwin, 1999; McCasland, 2005).

On the other hand, generation Y has been studied differently across boundaries with the cultural and behavioural differences (Howe & Strauss, 2000). This is also further supported by Syrett & Lammimam (2004) that the behaviours of generation Y varies due to social uncertainties due to the ideal studies point is not so direct. Hence, in these studies, the research is to conduct in Malaysia to understand from the perspective generation Y.

Purchase Intention

According to Fandos & Flavian (2006) and Halim & Hameed (2005), the intention of purchase is defined as the implied promise to one's self on buying the product again and again during the next trip to the market. Some of the scholars suggested that the purchase intentions are rooted from buying behaviour (Goyal, 2014). As purchase intention are crucial for the company in marketing and selling the products to the market for profit maximization, thus, the purchase intention related data would be able to guide the managers in the marketing decisions on product development, market segmentation as well as promotional strategies (Goyal, 2014). Besides that, the purchase intention also related to the purchasing behaviour (Morwitz & Schmittlein, 1992). This is further supported by Morwitz, Steckel and Gupta (1996) that there is a positive correlation between purchase intention and purchase behaviour. Purchase behaviour is referred to the action of buying by a consumer on particular products and their intention and willingness to purchase the product again (Blackwell et al, 2006). The current purchasing behaviour also refers to the time of purchase, amount purchased as well as the purchased product or service type (Mollehn & Wilson, 2010).

For generation Y, their attitude towards CSR products are one of the important aspects of purchase intensions. They feel that they have the moral obligation towards CSR products (Lee & Diddi, 2017). Moreover, CSR has a positive relationship on the current purchasing behaviour and future purchase intention as the consumers will evaluate the fulfilment of CSR in corporate activities (Aaker, 1996 and Esch et al., 2006). According to the research done by Boonpattarakan (2012), the awareness of the consumers on CSR will positively affect the chances of purchase for the companies' products or services. Thus, CSR has an impact on the purchase intention.

Corporate Social Responsibility

Corporate social responsibility (CSR) is first defined by Bowen (1953) as the responsibility of company on the consequences of actions in the wider perspective aside of just profit and loss. This is further supported by Ramasamy and Yeung that the organization should contributing by doing social good as part of responsibility to the society and environment apart of making profit. Next, the scope of CSR is further detailed into four hierarchy by Carroll (1991) as such there are economic, legal, ethical and philanthropic responsibility. Economic responsibility is defined as the monetary of the business; legal responsibility as in law and regulation compliance; ethical responsibility is focus on doing the right thing in fair and just ways by going beyond the laws to be integrity; philanthropic responsibility is the voluntary give and service back to the society (Carroll, 1991).

Later, Googins et al. (2007) further describe the state of CSR is in a "pre-paradigmatic stage where there is scant agreement on definitions and terms and no consensus has been reached about what it includes and does not include in its boundaries". This statement is further supported by the study of Deegan (2002) that CSR is beyond the motive of profit making but to focus on other aspect such as protect the environment, care for the employees' welfare, business ethical as well as social welfare. The extend of CSR involvement in the companies has expand according to time when the companies are more assured on the beneficial of CSR. For instance, the companies that involved in CSR will provide the social value to the consumers and portray a positive image as the responsible firm (Deegan, 2002). As such, the range of CSR could be of better performance, enhanced brand image and reputation, increase profit as well as attract and retain customers to achieve competitive advantages (Lingreen et al., 2009; Susniene & Sargunas, 2009). In the latest context, the CSR is still defined as the expression of firm's commitment on social and ethical responsibility to the society (Walliser & Scott, 2018).

Nevertheless, the CSR adoption and practise are varying geographically due to the differences in social, political and aspect across countries (Chapple & Moon, 2005; Kimber & Lipton, 2005). The studies further supported that the focus on the CSR activities are substantial from each country (Chapple & Moon, 2005; Maignan & Ralston, 2002, and Welford, 2005). Particularly, the CSR practise in Asian countries are lag behind by the Western countries (Ang, 2000; Low, 2004; Welford, 2004). However, Ramasamy and Ting (2005) studies has indicated that the CSR activities had been gaining public attention in Asia starting on 2004.

In Malaysia, CSR has been developed since year 1974. These are raised by several parties. As such, the Environmental Quality Act is introduced by the government to legislate the environmental safety and pollution issues. For instance, the act is introduced to instruct the construction firm to comply with the Environmental Impact Assessment (EIA) when developing new housing areas or any projects. Some non-governmental organizations (NGO) and media also raised concerns on the health hazards products, product safety, environmental pollution and discrimination against the handicapped people (Abdul, 2002). On year 2004, CSR is being widely promoted to both public and private companies through the establishment of Malaysian Institute of Integrity (IIM) under National Integrity Plan. It is aimed to promote the good practice of ethical principles, good values and integrity. Moreover, the perception of management and executives in the Malaysian firms are having a positive attitude towards the CSR. It is further indicated in the studies that the companies are viewing the benefit of CSR with the perspective on economical view of the business in maximizing the company's profit while expanding the non-economic and philanthropic dimension (Abdul, 2002). However, the real involvement of management and executives are still remaining low in Malaysia. This is due to there are some minimum standards of social and environmental responsibility that shareholders and stakeholders are demanding the firms to take responsibility for their products (Fisher, Turner, & Morling, 2009). As the increasing global competition and borderless markets growing stronger in the international platform, the study conducted by Altman (2007) has concluded that the corporations that do not equip with CSR activities will likely be left behind by the international corporations that has sound and strong CSR activities.

Besides that, the purchase intention is strongly influenced by the CSR activities (Smith, 2003; Castaldo, Perrini,

Misani, & Tencati, 2009), therefore, this research is done to understand the relationship between purchase intention and CSR in Malaysia, particularly among the generation Y.

CSR Awareness

In Malaysia, the CSR awareness has been raising due to the increased in the level of education as well as the media influence. Thus, the consumers are more aware of the purpose and existence of the business. Hence, the corporations have to be more aware of this CSR and care more about the society and environment. The study conducted by Rahim, et al (2011), the firm think that the degree of CSR involvement will have effect on the consumers' purchase intention. In the aspect of individual, the consumer think that CSR is related to the ethical awareness (Kaya, 2014). This is also supported by the study of Goi (2009) that the consumers are getting more aware and sensitive on the CSR conducted by the firm as the society becomes more affluent. They believe this will influence their buying decision and buying pattern.

The studies conducted by Mohr, Webb and Harris (2001) has showed that CSR has an effect on the consumers' attitudes and purchase behaviour. The research has showed a significant correlation between CSR and consumer responses. This also supported by the research done by Sen and Bhattacharya (2001) on the response of consumers towards the perception on CSR. The result has shown that CSR is able to directly affect the consumer purchase intention on the corporate's products.

Trust of CSR

According to the Oxford dictionary, trust is defined as the firm belief on the reliability, truth, or ability of someone or something (Oxford dictionary, 2012). According to Pivato, Misani, and Tencati (2008, p. 6), trust is "an expectation that the trustee is willing to keep promises and to fulfil the obligations." Therefore, research has indicated that the companies have to deliver the message on their CSR activities clearly to the consumers in a trustworthy way, as such through the official certification like ISO, widely-recognized eco labels and so on in order to let the consumer believe that they are responsible and trustable through rebranding from CSR (Mohr & Webb, 2005). This is also supported by former research that the socially responsible companies will be able to generate a greater trust in consumers through the trust in CSR (Maignan et al., 1999). The Ipsos research conducted from 1999 to 2008 also shown that consumers are trust a company with real commitment to societal actions (Swaen & Chumpitaz, 2008). The trust of CSR also extends towards the upstream of the industry whereby the consumers will have more confidence on the reliable suppliers if the suppliers are able to meet their social responsibility and comply to the obligations (Chaudhuri & Holbrook, 2001) as the consumers will have less doubt and more trust on the suppliers' moral commitment.

However, there are differences between conducting the CSR activities and the communication process. According to Geokhaji, 2015, the consumers are perceiving the CSR activities conducted by the companies as good, but the consumers are having a low trust on corporate communications. Nevertheless, they are less sceptical to the long-term companies' commitment to the specific issues or cause. On contrary, the consumers are also highly aware of the negative news on CSR in the companies. This is supported by the studies done by Sen and Bhattacharya (2001) and Mohr and Webb (2005). The consumers will react strongly to the firm that is social irresponsible, irresponsible behaviour or misleading message, which will affect the consumers to switch brand, create negative perception as well as influence the other consumers.

Therefore, the trust of CSR will be one of the determinants in this study as it will affect the purchase intention of the consumers.

Willingness to Pay Premium Price

Aguilar and Vlosky (2007) define a price premium as the amount of money an individual is willing to pay to secure a welfare improvement. The study also stated that the consumers will concerns on buying the differentiated products that provide a social and environmental standard. The differentiated products are often accompanied with the willingness to pay premium price (Loureiro & Lotade, 2005). There are studies also conducted to understand the attitudes toward differentiated products and willing to pay a higher price as well as understand how attitudes on the differentiated products transform into monetary values (Aguilar & Vlosky, 2007).

Some studies also have been discussed on the perception of high price for a product produced by socially responsible company and whether or the premium pricing is perceived to be fair (Crawford & Mathews, 2001; Bolton, Warlop & Alba., 2003; Xia, Monroe & Cox, 2004). While the consumers are willing to pay a premium price for the socially responsible products. They are buying only the best products at the best possible price. For the consumers' perspective, the price has a negative effect on purchase intention, but CSR products are able to reduce such negative impact (Edelman, 2014). Hence, it is up to the customers' sense of fairness on the price tag. When they are seeing the values of the products, they will perceive the price as fair (Xia et al., 2004).

Therefore, some studies also supported that it is more effective to increase the product value through marketing than price reduction to increase the purchase intention of consumers (Arora & Henderson, 2010). Besides that, the consumers also willing to pay for the product when they got to know the amount of purchase will be related to good cause (Chladek, Florack & Kleber, 2013). In addition, the study also indicated that the consumers will consider the CSR products as fair when they have trust on the company and will not think that the higher price on the CSR products are part of the financial strategy to increase the profit (Habel et al., 2016). Hence, the willingness to pay premium price will be one of the determinants in this study as it is important for the marketing strategy and planning.

Consumers' Awareness of CSR and Purchase Intention

There is a positive effect between the CSR and purchase intention (Lee & Shin, 2009). This is also related to the positive effect on the behavioural intentions of the consumers (Bhattacharya & Sen, 2004). This also related to the CSR awareness of the consumers. The study conducted by Tian et al. (2011) has indicated that the more the consumers are aware of the CSR activities, the more they are favouring towards the company. This is also supported by the research of Balcova (2012) on the consumers' purchase intentions which are affected by the meaning of CSR and concern on awareness. This also supported by the studies of Carvalho, Sen, Mota & Lima (2010), Mohr & Webb (2005), Alniacik, Alniacik & Genc (2011) on the positive relationship between CSR and purchase intention. Particularly, the study by Alniacik et al. (2011) also concern on the negative and positive perspective on the corporate social and environmental responsibility at which it able to demonstrate the positive information on CSR will increase the consumers' purchase intention.

In this study, millennials are the focus group as they are showing a higher level of awareness on CSR (Geokhaji, 2015), with female having a higher tendency towards CSR (Cone Communications & Echo, 2013). This is further describing that female consumers would not really clear on the ultimate impact of CSR marketed by the company but will still trying out their best way to save the world whenever step into a store (Cone Communications & Echo, 2013, p.60). Thus, separating further on the CSR perception of female and male.

Nevertheless, the research conducted by Sharma, 2014 showed the other way around as there is no significant relationship between CSR and purchase intention. Some studies also indicated that the CSR awareness might be an assumption or artificially induction (Mohr et al., 2001). Furthermore, the study also found out the CSR awareness is low and might limiting the consumers' ability to purchase due to the CSR is broadly define and with a complex context. Thus, it is hard for the company to ensure the fully understanding of the consumers (Sen & Bhattacharya, 2001).

Nasir et al. (2014) also reported that the lack of awareness and perception on CSR in Malaysia and supported by Geokhaji (2015) that the CSR awareness of the consumers are low, but the high educated individuals might be more aware on the CSR and play a role in their purchase intention.

Thus, the hypothesis is proposed as below.

Hypothesis 1: There is a significant relationship between CSR awareness and purchase intention among the generation Y in Malaysia.

Consumer's Trust of CSR and Purchase Intention

Trust of CSR play a crucial role in the consumers' purchase intention (Swaen & Chumpitaz, 2008). It would act of one of the key drivers for purchase intention. To gain the trust of CSR by the consumers, the company have to practise good corporate citizenship (Rahim et al., 2011). Through communication of CSR initiatives, companies seek to instil awareness, attitudes, identification, and trust within consumers and therefore positively influence consumers purchase intentions and company loyalty (Du, Bhattacharya, & Sen, 2010). Besides that, the company that are more active in the social arena to promote CSR and related activities, they would be high likely to be trusted, discussed and recommended by the consumers (Sharma, 2012). According to Pivato, Misani and Tencati (2008), the study also indicated that the CSR would be able to create the consumers' trust. The result also showed that company performance on the CSR would affect the consumer trust and the trust would be able to influence on consumers' action.

Nevertheless, there are findings resulted the other way that trust of CSR is this factor might have the least impact on the purchase intention (Balcova, 2012). Furthermore, the study conducted by Semuel and Chandra (2014) has stated that the CSR influence would only on the willingness to pay the premium price and do not have a significant effect between the trust of CSR and purchase intention in Surabaya. As the cross-cultural differences of CSR practices across the region, the acceptance of CSR might be varying and thus affecting the trust of the consumers on CSR practices. For example, the study conducted by Ray (2008) has indicated that the CSR practices in America are slightly more advance in pushing the corporate to adopt the CSR practices compared to China. As such, the American companies are more concern on teaching the CSR concept to the younger generation compared to Chinese companies.

Hence, the result might be differed in term of the CSR practices and acceptance of generation Y in Malaysia on CSR and thus able to trust it and trigger their purchase intention towards CSR products.

Thus, the hypothesis is proposed as below.

Hypothesis 2: There is a significant relationship between trust of CSR activities and purchase intention among the generation Y in Malaysia.

Willingness to Pay Premium Price and Purchase Intention

As the price has been reflected on the CSR products, thus, the studies have been done to understand the consumers' perspective. Thus, statistically, the willingness to pay premium price has been one of the significant factors on the purchase intention in the view of CSR products. The study conducted by Balcova (2012) has indicated that the consumers are price sensitive under the current economic condition but will still willing to pay more for the CSR products with justifiable price increase. They also feel that it is necessary and reasonable for the price to higher as the products or services are produced by the socially responsible company.

The studies conducted by Crawford & Mathews, (2001); Bolton et al., (2003) or Xia et al., (2004) also supporting on the above result. Furthermore, if the products are labelled clearly to be associated with a specific CSR activity that able to link to the consumers' personal beliefs, the consumers will tend to be more willing to pay for a premium price (Bhattacharya & Sen, 2004). Anselmsson and Johansson (2007) also conducted the study through qualitative, explorative and conceptual approach to further support that the consumers are willing to pay the premium price that related to the CSR. The relationship between the consumers' purchase intentions also showed to be related with the CSR engagement of an organization (Dodd & Supa, 2011).

From the study conducted by Zia, 2016, the finding shows that the CSR is a vital tool to allow the companies to charge a higher price. According to Aguilar and Vlosky (2007), the consumers also tend to respond positively to CSR products or services that link to the social and environmental stewardship, they are often willing to pay a premium for these products (Loureiro & Lotade, 2005; Govindasamy, DeCongelio, & Bhuyan, 2006). On average, about 46 percent of consumers in Europe report a willingness to pay more for ethical products (MORI, 2000: cited in De Pelsmacker, Driesen, & Rayp, 2006).

Nevertheless, there are studies showed that the consumers do not wish to pay for this premium price (Beckmann, 2007). Not all the consumers are willing to accept to pay more on CSR products (Bhattacharya & Sen, 2004; Mohr & Webb,

2005). The studies conducted on Mexican consumers also indicated that their main factor of buying will be based on price and not really concern on the CSR practices even being informed (Trapero, Lozada & Garcia, 2010). The study also showed that they acknowledged the importance of CSR but would not influence on their purchase intention. Hence, there are differences across study on this topic and have been partly contradicts with each other, which has indicating that the complexity and dynamics of CSR on the influences on consumers. Thus, the current study has to investigate further the target group of generation Y in Malaysia towards the CSR products and how this factor affects their purchase intention.

Thus, the hypothesis is proposed as below.

Hypothesis 3: There is a significant relationship between the willingness to pay premium price and purchase intention among the generation Y in Malaysia.

Research Framework

This study is adopting the model of Carroll (1979) and Tian et al. (2011) that focus mostly on CSR practices asides of just business responsibilities but also involve the philanthropic, ethical, and environmental activities.

The three variables that play a vital role in CSR for consumer relationship and thus has directly influence on the purchase intentions. These three variables are the consumers' awareness of CSR, consumers' trust in CSR and willingness to pay premium price.

It is proposed to study that these three factors would directly influence the purchase intention of the consumers in buying CSR products.

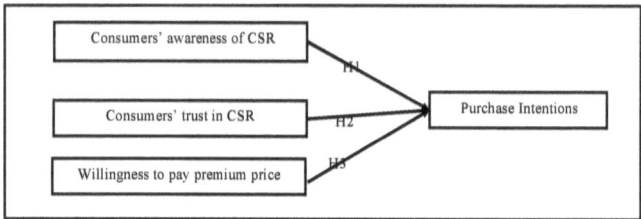

Figure 1.2 The research framework

Gaps of the Study

In this case, the research is conducted in Malaysia which is a developing country. CSR standards that initially generated in Europe and United States demand the application in developing countries as well as CSR has been successfully applied in developed countries. This research is conducted among the generation Y in Malaysia to fill in the gap that lack of the research have been done in Malaysia. In addition, the CSR can be used as a marketing tool to act as a competitive advantage in strengthening the business performance of the firm (Porter & Kramer 2006; Varadarajan & Menon 1988).

Therefore, this study is conducted to understand the impact of CSR on the purchase intention among generation Y in Malaysia to fill in the gaps that the particular focus group is studied as generation Y will be the current and future work force in all the industry.

CHAPTER 3

Procedures

The research approach, strategy and technique that are utilized on this research. This study explained on the adopted research design, population, sample size, and sampling techniques. This section also including the operationalization of the variables, the questionnaire and approach adapted for data collection. Lastly, this section has discussed on the approaches adopted in the data analysis.

Research Philosophy

Research philosophy is defined as the assumptions of researcher that made on the understanding of nature and advancement of knowledge, that focused on the research approach and strategies to achieve that development (Saunders, Lewis & Thornhill, 2009). There are two categories of research philosophy which are positivism paradigm and interpretive paradigm. The main variance between the categories are the differential in the concept on human beings as well as the method used in studying the human behaviour (Thomas, 2004).

For positivist philosopher, the researchers would believe that the actuality is exterior and objective. Instead of the subjective reflection and intuition approach to study on the social human behaviours, it would be to be studied through the objective methods due to the reality is external and objective (Easterby-Smith, Thorpe & Lowe, 2002). The researchers that practices positivism presume that humans behave naturally and having the characteristics that independent from the others (Thomas, 2004). Thus, the researchers are expected to act independently as what they believe on the human behaviours and use multiple hypotheses and deductions to sum up the human behaviours. Hence, to be able to produce the statistical results, the samples should be in a large group and thus able to make a probable quantifiable generalized concept (Easterby-Smith, Thorpe & Lowe, 2002).

In contrast for the constructionist concept, the actuality is presumed to be socially constructed and decided by human itself rather than the external and objective factors (Easterby-Smith, Thorpe & Lowe, 2002). Thus, the constructionist practitioners would try to digest the inferior concepts of human in relation to the reality (Thomas, 2004). This means that they are more concerned on how people think, feel and act with each other (Easterby-Smith, Thorpe & Lowe, 2002). Hence, the result would be produced from the observation and then induce a new theoretical concept. Therefore, the samples size would be relatively smaller group compared with the positivist practitioners, because the type of research would be focus deeply to understand on a specific topics or situation and thus able to induce a new abstraction (Easterby-Smith, Thorpe & Lowe, 2002).

Thus, the choice of the research paradigm depends not only the researcher's philosophical thinking but mainly on the nature of subject being researched, and the questions being addressed. In this study, based on the research questions and objectives, the quantitative approach of the positivist paradigm is best suited for the adoption in this research as it is more focused on the behaviours of large group to produce the statistical probable generalized results.

Research Design

Research could be conducted in different ways, as such descriptive, exploratory and explanatory research (Bickman & Rog, 2008). As the aim of this study is to describe how CSR effect on the purchase intention among generation Y in Malaysia. Thus, this study has adopted the descriptive approach through online questionnaire survey. The descriptive research means that the research is done to study the population attitudes, behaviours and characteristics (Bickman & Rog, 2008), as well as to understand a particular pattern and scenario (Saunders et al., 2009).

As the current research are rooted from the wide range study of CSR which have been carried out through the deductible manner (Bryman & Bell, 2013), thus, the former constructed conceptual framework should be adopted as a reference and basis to conduct the current research so that it allows the discovery of more possible outcomes from the existing theory and reality. Hence, the inductive method is not adopted as such approach is more appropriate for researches to explore new concepts and new results that deduce from the population (Bryman & Bell, 2007).

There are two different time zone for research which are the cross-sectional study, that defined as the snapshot of the study at a particular time and the longitudinal study, that defined as the study of an event over a given period of time. As this research is adopting the descriptive approach in deductible manner, thus the cross-sectional time zone study is selected. Besides that, cross-sectional study is majority done for survey purpose (Bryman, 2007). Furthermore, it is less time consuming and able to picture a better of data collection on the variables in a snapshot of time, compared to longitudinal study (Saunders et al., 2012).

Population and Sampling

As the research is done to collect the view of the consumers through survey approach, thus, the questionnaire survey will be adopted in this study. The target audience for the survey is the Malaysian's generation Y aged between 20 to 35 years old. As the study aimed to study the purchase intention of the generation Y that is the next line for the consumption group for the economy, thus, the age of 20 years old and above are accounted as they are more mature and have a higher consuming power.

To accommodate the aim of this research, the convenience sampling technique are adopted for the data collection. Convenience sampling is a statistical approach for illustrating a big representative group of participants through volunteering basis due to the easier accessibility (Business Dictionary). Thus, this technique is quicker in collecting data due to the volunteering basis. However, it is harder to ensure the representativeness of the population and thus large group of respondents are needed. Next, the research would be based on the input from the volunteers which might be biased. However, the larger sample size can reduce such biasness.

As Malaysia is having about 9.3millions of generation Y aged between 20 to 35 (Refer to Table 2.1), thus, according to the research conducted by Taherdoost (2017), the representative sampling size for more than 1,000,000 people of population, the samples size should be at least 384 to achieve the confident level of 95%. Thus, in this study, a sum of 385 consumers have been randomly selected as the respondents. The questionnaires are distributed to the generation Y in Malaysia via social media approach through Internet. As the social network are used, thus the targeted audience would be required to fill in an online questionnaire for this study. Questionnaires also shared through personal contact as well as posted in groups that comprised mostly of generation Y.

Instrumentation Measurement

The questionnaire comprised of two major parts at which the first part is to collect the socio-demographic information of the respondents that used to describe the target participants while the second part is subdivided into five sub-sections to collect the data for the study. The first part of the questions is collected the data for gender, age, ethnicity, education level and income level. The gender of the representative is taken into the study as different gender would behave differently to the CSR practices, at which female tend to be having a higher tendency towards CSR (Cone Communications & Echo, 2013). Age is to ensure the generation Y is taking the test. The data for ethnicity, education level and income level to identify on the relationship that might affected on the CSR awareness as well as their purchase intention.

While, the first sub-sections of the second part of the questionnaire is used to collect the data on the background information of the respondents on the understanding about the CSR. It covers the self-evaluation question on the familiarity on the CSR concept, the issues related to the CSR practices, as well as the consumers' awareness of the companies that behaved social responsibly based on the model of Bilikova (2015). All the results including the unaware of the CSR concepts are captured and included as part of the variables in data analysis.

Second sub-section of the second part has covered on the in-depth awareness questions adapted from Salmones et al. (2005) and Perex and Rodriguez del Bosque (2013). The 5-point Likert scale is used, so that the range of the consumers' awareness are able to be measured in data analysis.

The third sub-section of the second part has covered the trust of CSR among the generation Y. The questions are adapted from Newell and Goldsmith (2001) and Erdem and Swait (2004). This section's main aim to obtain the basic understanding of the consumers' trust on the socially responsible companies in Malaysia and their CSR activities, initiatives and projects.

The forth sub-section of the second part is to gather the information on the consumers' willingness to pay premium price for CSR products/services. The questionnaire also included the explanation on the CSR products that adopted from Etile & Teyssier, 2012). This sub-section's questions are taken from Garcia-Conde, Maring and Maya (2016). The key result for this sub-section is to figure out the behavioural effect on the increased price on CSR product perceived by consumers.

The fifth sub-section of the second part is used to study the purchase intention of the consumers. The questions are adapted from Mulaessa and Wang (2016). The key reason for this survey to identify the relationship of the consumers' behaviours on the company that practices CSR activities.

For the second part, the five-point Likert scale are adapted from sub-section two to sub-section five. The Likert scale is ranged from "1" for "strongly disagree" to "5" for "strongly agree" in order to express the degree of agreement or disagreement with each of a series of questions in this survey (Malhotra, 2007).

The data obtained are studied through SPSS software and analysed using descriptive and multiple linear regression statistics. Descriptive statistics are used to study the socio-demographic data like gender, age, ethnicity, education level and income level of the representatives. Below listed the Table 3.1 for the survey items and constructs.

Data Collection and Analysis

The data collected are analysed through SPSS software. The data are coded and entered the SPSS software and analysed through three stages. Firstly, the socio-demographic information of the respondents is generated to understand the background and characteristics of the respondents. Next, the data also processed for the reliability test to check on the result of the Cronbanch's alpha coefficient. Lastly, the third stage would involve the analysis using correlation and multi-linear regression analysis.

Validity

Validity refers to degree of which the data collection method able to achieve
the objectives of the study and the degree of which the research findings to achieve the aim of the research (Saunders, Lewis & Thornhill, 2009).

Table 3.1: Survey Items and Constructs

Survey Item		Literature
Variable 1: Consumer Awareness of Corporate Social Responsibility (CSR)		
1.1	I care about environmental protection.	Tian, 2011
1.2	I pay attention to social issues.	Tian, 2011
1.3	I buy quality and /or inexpensive products, regardless of whether the provider is socially responsible or not.	Tian, 2011
1.4	I think that corporations play responsible roles in society.	Salmones et al., 2005
Variable 2: Consumer's trust in CSR		
2.1	I think a company's socially responsible actions sincerely contribute to Malaysia.	Keh and Xie, 2009
2.2	I think companies take a lot of effort to be socially responsible.	Keh and Xie, 2009
2.3	I think a company's socially responsible practises can make a substantial contribution to Malaysia.	Keh and Xie, 2009
2.4	I view companies that practise CSR in a more positive manner.	Keh and Xie, 2009
Variable 3: Willingness to pay premium price for CSR products		
3.1	I am willing to buy CSR product even though choices are limited.	Voon, Ngui & Agrawal, 2011
3.2	I am willing to buy CSR products because the benefits outweigh the cost.	Voon, Ngui & Agrawal, 2011
3.3	Buying CSR product is the right thing to do even if they cost more.	Voon, Ngui & Agrawal, 2011

3.4	I don't mind spending more time sourcing for CSR product.	Voon, Ngui & Agrawal, 2011
3.5	I would still buy CSR product even though conventional alternatives are on sale.	Voon, Ngui & Agrawal, 2011
Dependent Variable: Purchase Intention		
4.1	I will purchase a product because the company pays attention to charity activities.	Espejel et al., 2008
4.2	I would pay more to buy products from a socially responsible corporation.	Poemring & Dolniar, 2009
4.3	If the price and quality of two products are the same, I would buy from the firm with a socially responsible reputation.	Poemring & Dolniar, 2009
4.4	I will return to purchase a product again if the company has strong society responsibility.	Poemring & Dolniar, 2009

In relationship to the questionnaire survey methods, there are two types of validity should be done which are the content and construct validity. As the questionnaires are adapted based on numerous studies, thus, the content and construct validity would be satisfied from the results obtained from the sampling collection (Creusen, Hultink & Eling, 2012).

Reliability

Reliability is the consistency in achieving the same outcome with the data calculation are done repeatedly multiple times. Reliability refers to the consistency of a measure. A test is reliable if the result is consistent repeatedly. It is the degree to which an instrument will give similar results for the same individuals at different times. In this research, reliability test will be used to test the consistency of the result from the questionnaire. To reduce biasness, the respondents are treated as anonymous (Saunders, Lewis & Thornhill,

2009). Cronbach's alpha is the most common measure of internal consistency. In order to ensure the test is reliable, Cronbach's alpha value has to be more than 0.7 (Nunnaly, 1978). This value provides an overall reliability coefficient for a set of variables.

Inferential Statistics

Inferential statistics able to identify the patterns and assumption based on the collected data and make a conclusion (Oxford Dictionary). It able to generalize the population results obtained from the collected data and present the assumptions to generalize the population pattern and behaviors. There are inferential tools that use in this research are the Pearson coefficient correlation and the multiple regression analysis.

Pearson Coefficient of Correlation

Pearson coefficient of correlation is the most common measure of "predictability". It is to measure and test the relationships between variables. The relation will be found when the correlation is computed but we will not be able to say that one variable can actually causes changes in another variable. The ρ-value use to evaluate whether there is a linear relationship between the two variables in the population. The positive and negative sign is to indicate the direction of relationship between two tested variables. There are two assumptions has to be made when conducting Pearson coefficient of correlation analysis which the first is the variables are bivariate normally distributed. Secondly, the data should be a random sampling from the population. The score on each variable obtained should be independent of each other. In this research, Pearson coefficient of correlation is used to test the relationship between CSR awareness, trust of CSR and willingness to pay premium price and purchase intention among generation Y in Malaysia.

Two hypotheses are proposed as below:

$H0: \rho = 0$ *("the population correlation coefficient is 0; there is no association")*

$H1: \rho \neq 0$ *("the population correlation coefficient is not 0; a nonzero correlation could exist")*

Four Conditions Prior To Multiple Regression

There are four conditions prior to multiple regression analysis, which are the normality test, linearity test, homoscedasticity test, and multicollinearity test.

Normality Test

Normality is crucial for multivariate analysis. It is based on the predictions that each variable and all the linear combination of these variables are normally distributed. Normality is evaluated through statistical or graphical methods. The statistical components are Skewness and Kurtosis, while the graphical method is Q-Q plots. Skewness is the symmetry of the distribution whereas kurtosis is the "peakedness" of the distribution. According to Yu and Meyer

(2006), values of less than 1.0 for skewness and kurtosis indicated that it is not violating the assumption of normality. The graphical observation of historical residual plot will be also be used to assess normality assumptions. A normally distributed date will have the shaped of bell curve while all the bars of the histogram on the middle. It did not skew either too much to the right or too much to the left (Hair, Anderson, Tatham and Black, 2010). It should be noted that the relationship between independent and dependent variables must be linear (Schneider, Math, Hommel & Blettner, 2010). If non-linear relationship exists, the actual strength of the relationships would be underestimated.

Linearity Test

Linearity test able to serve as an assumption for multiple regressions is to present the extent to which the change in the dependent variable is related with the independent variable. It shows the degree to which association between variables is in straight line. Linearity able to rectify on the data which is vital for regression analysis. It is also assumed that the multiple regression is based on the linearity of multivariate relationship, therefore, it is vital to analyse on the linearity of the data (Hair et al, 2010). Linearity can be examined by looking at the residual plots. A visual examination of the residual plot will show a rough straight line and not a curve.

Homoscedasticity Test

Homoscedasticity exists when the differences of the dependent variable is estimated to be the same at varies levels of the independent variables. This assumed based on the dependent variable (Hair et al, 2010). Homoscedasticity assumed that the dependent variable has to exhibit an equal level of variance, compared to the range of independent variables. It can be investigated through the visual inspection of the scatter plot of residuals.

Multicollinearity Test

Multicollinearity is the degree to which independent variables are highly correlated with one another. It is the degree to which a variable could be related to another variable in an analysis. It can have devastating effect on the regressions to the extend rendering them useless and even highly misleading. This is because when the independent variables are closely correlated with each other and the correlation values exceed 0.90. A high degree of correlation among independent variables reduces their predictive power (Hair et al, 2010). To test for multicollinearity in this study, a Pearson Product-Moment test will be performed. Collinearity statistics such as tolerance values and variance inflation factor (VIF) for the independent variables are calculated to determine whether multicollinearity problem exits with the data. Tolerance value ranges from zero to one where value of one indicates that the variable is not correlate with each other whereas, value of zero means the other round, which is the variable are fully correlated. When the tolerance value of less than 0.10, it means the present of multicollinearity in the independent variables. In contrast, the variance inflation factor (VIF) is the opposite of tolerance value with VIF close to or equal to one indicate that it is little or zero multicollinearity. Thus, the lower the value, away from 10, the better the VIF is. To conclude, tolerance value should be not less than 0.1 while VIF should not be greater than 10.

Multiple Regression Analysis

The objective of doing multiple regression analysis is to investigate on the association between the independent and dependent variables. It is one of the fundamental approaches in scientific study for allowing determination of significant association between independent and dependent variables (Bargiela, Nakashima and Pedrycz, 2005). It is also a statistical approach that used to assume one's score on a variable over the fundamental score of other variables.

The regression will be measured in a beta that gives a meaningful explanation on the association between independent and dependent variables. The beta might be positive or negatives that gives the degree of how much more increment or reduction for a dependent variable to a unit of difference in the independent variables. The regression result will be formulated in correlation coefficient (r), coefficient of determination (R^2), and adjusted coefficient of determination (adjusted R^2). These algebras would be used to represent how well the independent variable predict the dependent variable. The coefficient of determination (R^2) symbolic the extent of differences from the independent variable. Hence, the R square (R^2) represents the percentage of the total variation in the dependent variable values contributed to, or described by, the independent variable in a regression equation (Mendenhall & Sincich, 1989). The F value is used to evaluate the overall functionality of the regression model in analysing, predicting, or explaining the variation in the dependent variable (Bohrnstedt & Knoke, 1994).

Thus, the multiple regression analysis is used to discover the observed degree of the relationship between all three independent variables, the awareness of CSR, consumer's trust on CSR and willingness to pay premium price with the purchase intention among generation Y in Malaysia.

The multiple regression equation is as below:

$$Y = a + b_1X_1 + b_2X_2 + b_3X_3 + \ldots + b_nX_n + \epsilon$$

Where Y = dependent variable
a = Y intercept of the regression model
b = the slope of the regression model
X = the independent variables
ϵ = error

CHAPTER 4

Discovery

This section reveals the findings between dependent variables (Purchase Intention) and the independent variables (Consumers' Awareness of CSR, Consumers' Trust in CSR and Willingness to Pay Premium Price) for the target participants of Generation Y in Malaysia are discussed. Next this chapter demonstrated the collected data analysis and results which includes the descriptive statistics analysis, regression results, diagnostic checking on the validity and reliability of the data.

Descriptive Statistics

In this section, the demographic characteristics of the respondents are studied through the gender, age group, ethnicity, educational level and income level in the form of Table 4.1 as below. It is important to identify the background of the target group in order to understand how their background might influence on their interests towards CSR products and thus affecting their purchase intention on CSR products.

As there are about 32 million Malaysian as of 2018, thus, it is interested to find out that there were over 9 million of generation Y from aged 20 to 35 in Malaysia. There were 385 data collected from these target audiences, at which in particularly, the age range is identified. From the Table 4.1 below demonstrated that there are 35% of respondents are comprised of age from 21 to 25.

There are 46% respondents are from aged 26 to 30, which are the mid-age of the group and the higher consuming power than the previous age group as most of them are entering into the workforce. While there are 19% respondents are from the age of 31 to 35. The data collected are in relative to the data reported by the

Table 4.1 Demographic Profile

	Respondents	%
Age		
21-25	136	35%
26-30	176	46%
31-35	73	19%
Gender		
Male	145	38%
Female	240	62%
Ethnicity		
Malay	180	47%
Chinese	170	44%
India	20	5%
Others	15	4%
Educational Level		
SPM	11	3%
A-Levels/STPM/Pra-U	10	3%
Diploma	24	6%
Undergraduate	190	49%
Postgraduate	137	36%
PhD	13	3%
Income Level		
Below RM1000	71	18%
RM1001-RM2000	56	15%
RM2001-RM3000	90	23%
RM3001-RM4000	79	21%
RM4001-RM8000	73	19%
Above RM8001	16	4%

1. I think I am familiar with the concept of Corporate Social Responsibility.	Strongly Disagree	Disagree	Neutral	Agree	Strongly Agree
Number of Respondents	26	37	91	128	103
Percentage	7%	9%	24%	33%	27%
2. Which of the following issues are addressed by Corporate Social Responsibility					
Organizational Governance				182	47%
Human Rights				249	65%
Labour Practices				172	45%
Environment				264	69%
Fair Operating Practices				154	40%
Consumer Issues				180	47%
Community Involvement and Development				285	74%
3. Are you aware of any companies operating in Malaysia that can be considered socially responsible?				Yes	No
Number of Respondents				267	118
Percentage				69%	31%

Malaysian Department of Statistic, whereby there are a greater number of populations aged between 26 to 30.

Refer to the above Table 4.1, the result has showed that there are estimated 16.7 million of male and 15.7 million of female in Malaysia which make the ratio at 107 males per 100 females. On contrary, there are higher number of data collected from female respondents at the number of 240 (62%) compared to male respondents at the number of 145 (38%).

From the collected result shown in Table 4.1, there are higher number of Malay respondents at 47%, Chinese respondents at 44%, India at 5% and Other races at 4%. As the survey is conducted through convenience sampling, the result would still reflect for the major Malay at a higher ratio than other races, but there are more Chinese respondents which might indicate that the Chinese might be in a higher interest than Malay in this study or the research topic of CSR.

The educational background of each respondents is identified as it might indicate that their level study towards the interest on CSR. From the data presented in Table 4.1 has showed that majority of the respondents are undergraduate at 49%, the second highest score is postgraduate at 36%, Diploma at 6%, PhD at 3%, SPM at 3% and A-level/STPM/Pra-U at 3%. The collected data has showed a majority of the undergraduate among the generation Y, which is reflected through the increasing rate of Malaysia's Gross Enrolment Ratio from 14% in 1980 to 44% in 2016. Thus, the improvement of the Malaysia Higher Education has significantly shifted the education level from secondary education or pre-U to undergraduate (Star, May 6, 2018). It is also reported that the Higher Education Ministry secretary-general, Tan Sri Dr Noorul Ainur Mohd Nur delivered the inspiration to achieve best higher education hub in the world as stated Malaysia Higher Education Blueprint (2015-2025) in the Going Global 2018 conference, in order to produce more intellectual and holistic graduates. Thus, there would be higher number of undergraduate and postgraduate respondents that reflecting this trend.

From the Table 4.1 shown that the income level of the collected 385 data are almost evenly distributed among each income level, as such the income level from RM2001 to RM3001 has showed slightly higher at 23%, followed by income level of RM3001 to RM4000 at 21%, RM4001 to RM8000 at 19%, below RM1000 at 18%, RM1001 to RM2000 at 15% and lastly above RM8001 at 4%.

The income level will impact on the purchase intention of generation Y for their consumption behaviour towards CSR products as there are more spare money to spend. Although the education level is comprised mostly of undergraduate, but there are differences on the salary earned by each Malaysian generation Y, which might due to the differences in occupation and industry pursued. According to the Department of Statistic Malaysia, the median household income of T20 is at least RM13,148, while M40 is at RM6,275 while B40 is RM3,000. Thus, as the generation Y is newly joined to the workforce or have been working for few years, thus, it is able to find that most the respondents are earning between RM2001 to RM4000.

The survey has covered on the understanding of respondents towards corporate social responsibility amongst Generation Y in Malaysia. According to Table 4.1, there are three questionnaires being asked. The first question has sought the feedback of the familiarity of Malaysian generation Y on the concept of CSR. It is identified that most of the respondents are thinking that they are strongly familiar to CSR, which contributed to 27% of strongly agree and 33% of agree to the statement. 24% of the respondents are neutral to the statement. About 16% of the respondents are thinking that they are not familiar with the CSR concept which yield of 9% of disagree and 7% of strongly disagree to the statement.

The second question being asked was the selection of the issues that are addressed by corporate social responsibility. Most of the respondents are thinking that community involvement and development are addressed by CSR which yield a 74%. Environment issues are voted 264 times and contribute to 69%. The third issues that concerned by generation Y is the human rights which being selected 249 times and give a 65%. Both organizational governance and consumer issues are selected by 47% of the respondents while labour practices at 45%. The lowest vote is the fair operating practices which being voted by 40% of the respondents. These might signify that the issues that highly concerned by the Malaysian generation Y whom think that it would be addressed through corporate social responsibility.

The third question was the awareness of any companies operating in Malaysia that can be considered as socially responsible. From the result gathered through the survey, it is found that there are 267 Malaysian generation Y are aware of this which gives a 69% compared to the rest of the 31% or 118 respondents that are not aware.

In a nutshell, this indicated that majority of the Malaysian generation Y are quite familiar with the CSR concept and concern on the CSR issues related to community involvement and development, environment and human rights. They are also highly aware of companies that operating in Malaysia can be considered socially responsible.

Reliability Test

The reliability test was conducted to evaluate the consistency of the data that free from error. It is measured using Cronbach's Alpha coefficient (Zikmund, 2003). The Cronbach's Alpha coefficient for the three independent variables, such as consumers' awareness of CSR, consumers' trust in CSR as well as willingness to pay premium price with the independent variable, purchase intention has been measured using SPSS and listed in below Table 4.2.

From the Table 4.2 shown above, the questions being used in the survey questionnaire were reliable as per adopted by previous literature study as these questions were verified through factor analysis in validity assurance. From the result compiled from the SPSS tool demonstrated that all the items are above 0.70, which is the Cronbach alpha's coefficient, thus these collected data are acceptable and reliable for further inferential statistics test, which are multiple regression analysis. The overall

Table 4.2 Reliability Test on the variables used in this study

Variables	Number of Items	Cronbach Alpha
Consumers' awareness of CSR	4	0.802
Consumers' trust in CSR	4	0.762
Willingness to pay premium price	5	0.898
Purchase Intention	4	0.801

Cronbach alpha for all the variables is 0.717 which the sum of total items in each variable.

Inferential Statistics

Inferential statistics able to generalize the population results obtained from the collected data and present the assumptions to generalize the population pattern and behaviors. From the simple statistics result, the mean, variance and standard deviation of each variable are compiled.

Table 4.3 Compiled of mean, variance and standard deviation of each variables.

Name of Variable	Mean	Variance	Standard Deviation
Consumers' awareness of CSR	11.888	2.777	1.666
Consumers' trust in CSR	11.769	4.012	2.003
Willingness to pay premium price	17.057	15.252	3.905
Purchase Intention	15.478	8.031	2.834

The mean of each variables reflects the respondents' attitudes on answering the questionnaire. The variance is a measurement of the deviation points from the mean of the data. It is able to measure how much difference between the mean and the observation data. The standard deviation is defined as how well the mean represents the data (Field, 2000). In this result, the variance and standard deviation are very close to the mean.

As shown in the Table 4.3, the mean of the willingness to pay premium price giving a higher impact compared to other independent variables, which infer that generation Y in Malaysia are having a premium price concern. Whereas, consumers' trust in CSR has a lower mean indicated that generation Y have to first be aware to the products and take time to build their trust in order to increase their purchase intention.

Pearson coefficient of correlation

Pearson coefficient of correlation measures the strength and direction of the linear relationship between pairs of continuous variables in the population. It is measured against with the population correlation coefficient, ρ. From the test, it is able to determine on the statistically significant linear relationship between the variables, its strength of the linear relationship as in how close the relationship to the straight-line plot as well as the direction of the linear relationship as in increasing or decreasing. Nevertheless, it is only able to determine the association among the variables and do give inference on the causation.

Therefore, to test the hypothesis that the independent variables are associate with the dependent variable, the two-tailed significance test are adopted and the hypothesis are proposed as below:

H_0: ρ = 0 *("the population correlation coefficient is 0; there is no association")*
H_1: ρ ≠ 0 *("the population correlation coefficient is not 0; a nonzero correlation could exist")*

From the output result, it is demonstrated that there are correlations between each variable, with correlation is significant at the 0.01 level for the two-tailed test. Particularly, this test is to identify the association between the independent variables and dependent variables, thus listed as below. The Pearson correlation coefficient for consumers' awareness of CSR and purchase intention is 0.236 which is significant (ρ< 0.001 for two-tailed test), based on 385 collected data;

The Pearson correlation coefficient for consumers' trust in CSR and purchase intention is 0.411 which is significant (ρ< 0.001 for two-tailed test), based on 385 collected data; The Pearson correlation coefficient for willingness to pay premium price and purchase intention is 0.691 which is significant (ρ< 0.001 for two-tailed

Table 4.4 Pearson Correlation test on the variables used in this study

		SumofCA	SumofCT	SumofWP	SumofPI
SumofCA	Pearson Correlation	1	0.393**	0.278**	0.236**
	Sig. (2-tailed)		0.000	0.000	0.000
	N	385	385	385	385
SumofCT	Pearson Correlation	0.393**	1	0.421**	0.411**
	Sig. (2-tailed)	0.000		0.000	0.000
	N	385	385	385	385
SumofWP	Pearson Correlation	0.278**	0.421**	1	0.691**
	Sig. (2-tailed)	0.000	0.000		0.000
	N	385	385	385	385
SumofPI	Pearson Correlation	0.236**	0.411**	0.691**	1
	Sig. (2-tailed)	0.000	0.000	0.000	
	N	385	385	385	385

** Correlation is significant at the 0.01 level (2-tailed).

The consumers' awareness of CSR is denoted as SumofCA, the consumers' trust in CSR is denoted as SumofCT as well as willingness to pay premium price is denoted as SumofWP, while the dependent variable, Purchase intention is denoted as SumofPI.

test), based on 385 collected data. In conclusion, the null hypothesis is rejected while the hypothesis H_1: $\rho \neq 0$ ("the population correlation coefficient is not 0; a nonzero correlation could exist") is accepted as all the independent variables are having a statistically significant linear relationship (ρ< 0.001) with dependent variables.

Four Conditions Prior to Multiple Regression

There are four conditions prior to multiple regression analysis, which are the normality test, linearity test, homoscedasticity test, and multicollinearity test. Hence, the data are run using SPSS to valid these four conditions.

Normality Test

Normality Test allows the researcher to evaluate the normally distributed of the data. There are two hypotheses proposed below to evaluate the distribution for the data.

H_0: *The data is normally distributed.*
H_1: *The data is not normally distributed.*

According to Yu and Meyer (2006), values of less than 1.0 for skewness and kurtosis indicated that it is not violating the assumption of normality. Besides that, to be considered as normal univariate distribution, the study from George and Mallery (2010) also stated that the values for skewness and kurtosis should be between -2 and +2. From the Table 4.5 below demonstrated that the skewness and kurtosis of each independent and dependent variables are fulfilling the criterion of less than 1 and between -2 and +2. Thus, the null hypothesis is accepted that the data is normally distributed.

Table 4.5 The skewness and kurtosis of each variables

		SumofCA	SumofCT	SumofWP	SumofPI
N	Valid	385	385	385	385
	Missing	0	0	0	0
Skewness		-0.087	-0.422	-0.102	-0.191
Std. Error of Skewness		0.124	0.124	0.124	0.124
Kurtosis		-0.401	0.324	-0.112	-0.306
Std. Error of Kurtosis		0.248	0.248	0.248	0.248

Besides that, the normality of the data also evaluated using graphical method. The graphical observation of historical residual plot is used to assess normality assumptions. The data are plotted in the histogram have demonstrated the pattern of bell-shaped curve. Below figure showed that the data are plotted in bar and showing the pattern of bell-shaped with not skew too much to the right or left, except for the variable, consumers' trust in CSR.

In overall, the assumption for the normality of the data are still fulfilled as the assumption of normality is not violated using statistical method. Thus, the relationship between independent and dependent variables are linear. This is the first assumption that meet the condition for multiple regression analysis whereby each variable and all the linear combination of the variables are normally distributed.

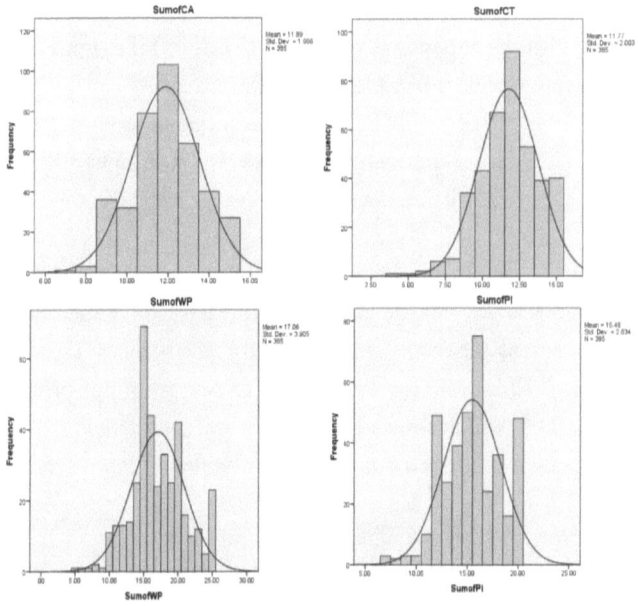

Figure 4.1 The data are plotted in histogram to demonstrated the bell-shaped of the graph for normality test.

Linearity Test

The second assumption is the linearity test to which required prior the multiple regression analysis. This analysis is based on the linearity of multivariate relationship. Hence, there are two tests conducted using SPS to confirm on the linearity of the data, through the ANOVE analysis on the significant value deviate from linearity and the standardized residual plot.

There are two hypotheses listed as below to evaluate the linearity of the data.

H_0: The relationship between the independent variables with the dependent variables are linear if the significant value deviate from linearity>0.05.

H_1: The relationship between the independent variables with the dependent variables are not linear if the significant value deviate from linearity<0.05.

From the Table 4.6 shown below demonstrated that the significant value deviate from linearity for consumers' awareness of CSR is 0.435>0.05; for consumers' trust in CSR is 0.737>0.05; for willingness to pay premium price is 0.438>0.05, which showed that all the independent variables are having a linear relationship with the dependent variable.

Table 4.6 The linearity test on each independent and dependent variable

			Sum of Squares	df	Mean Square	F	Sig.
SumofPI* SumofCA	Between Groups	(Combined)	224.369	8	28.046	3.688	0.000
		Linearity	171.450	1	171.450	22.543	0.000
		Deviation from Linearity	52.918	7	7.560	0.994	0.435
	Within Groups		2859.694	376	7.606		
	Total		3084.062	384			

			Sum of Squares	df	Mean Square	F	Sig.
SumofPI* SumofCT	Between Groups	(Combined)	568.085	11	51.644	7.656	0.000
		Linearity	521.788	1	521.788	77.356	0.000
		Deviation from Linearity	46.297	10	4.630	0.686	0.737
	Within Groups		2515.978	373	6.745		
	Total		3084.062	384			

			Sum of Squares	df	Mean Square	F	Sig.
SumofPI* SumofWP	Between Groups	(Combined)	1553.705	20	77.685	18.478	0.000
		Linearity	1472.311	1	1472.311	350.194	0.000
		Deviation from Linearity	81.394	19	4.284	1.019	0.438
	Within Groups		1530.357	364	4.204		
	Total		3084.062	384			

The residual plot also being constructed using SPSS as shown in figure below. The residual plot compared the observed cumulative distribution function of the standardized residual to the expected cumulative distribution function of the normal distribution. Hence, it is able to conclude that the data is normally distributed as well as disperse along the straight line and thus indicated that the data is linearly in the multivariate relationship. This fulfilled the second assumption for the multiple regression analysis on the linearity of the data.

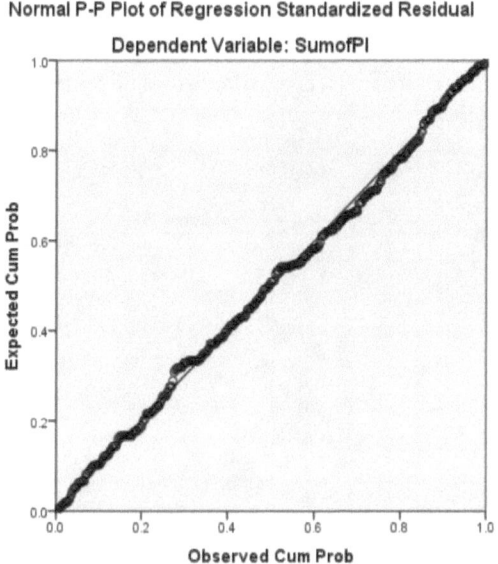

Figure 4.2 The residual plot to demonstrate the distribution data along the straight line.

Homoscedasticity Test

Homoscedasticity test is conducted to ensure the homogeneity of variance. This indicated that the variance around the regression is equal to all values of the independent variables. This test is to assumes that across the range of independent variables, the dependent variable exhibits equal level of variance. Thus, based on the figure below demonstrated that the scatterplot of the residuals. The data are dispersed more uniformity and as the independent value increase along the X-axis, the variation in the residuals are roughly similar, thus, it is still slight to be homoscedastic. Thus, this homoscedasticity is slight fulfilled the third assumption as it is based on the visual judgemental on the scatterplot.

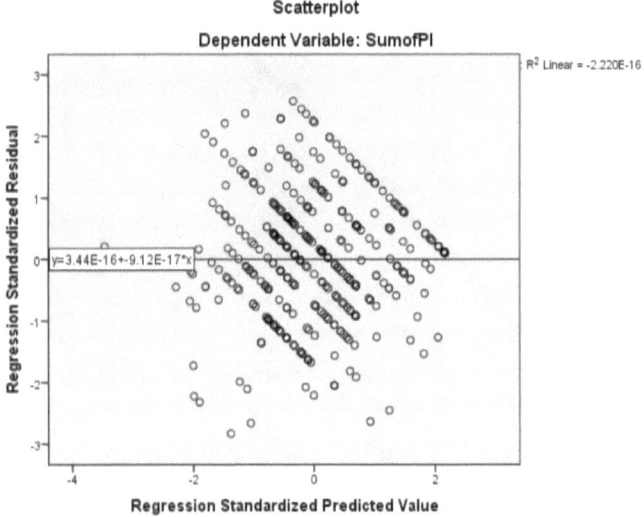

Figure 4.3 The scatterplot for homoscedasticity test.

Multicollinearity Test

Multicollinearity is vital to check the interrelation of each independent variable. From the Table 4.7 below, the collinearity statistics has demonstrated that the tolerance level of each independent variable are more than 0.1 and less than 1. The tolerance level of the consumers' awareness of CSR is 0.1<0.831<1; the consumers' trust in CSR is 0.1<0.740<1 and willingness to pay premium price is 0.1<0.808<1. Thus, it is indicated that all the variables have no correlation with other variables and do not have the present of multicollinearity issues. This test also checked on the variance inflation factor (VIF) whereby it should be opposite of the tolerance value by closer to one to demonstrated little or no multicollinearity. The rule of thumb is that VIF should not be greater than 10. From the Table 4.7 below shown that, the VIF of consumers' awareness of CSR is 1.204 <10; the consumers' trust in CSR is 1.351<10; and willingness to pay premium price is 1.238<10. Hence, this data fulfilled the forth assumption for multiple regression analysis whereby the independent variables are not closely correlated with each other.

Table 4.7 The result on collinearity statistics

Model	Unstandardized Coefficients B	Unstandardized Coefficients Std. Error	Standardized Coefficients Beta	t	Sig.	Collinearity Statistics Tolerance	Collinearity Statistics VIF
(Constant)	5.199	0.832		6.249	0.000		
SumofCA	0.007	0.068	0.004	0.105	0.917	0.831	1.204
SumofCT	0.205	0.060	0.145	3.424	0.001	0.740	1.351
SumofWP	0.456	0.029	0.629	15.521	0.000	0.808	1.238

a. Dependent Variable: SumofPI

Multiple Regression Analysis

As all the four assumptions prior to multiple regression analysis are fulfilled, the ANOVA analysis is conducted to measure the significant of each independent variable on the dependent variables. In the multiple regression analysis, it able to report the overall p-value, overall R square, and the beta value for each independent variable. From this test, the result able to discover the observed degree of the relationship between all three independent variables, the awareness of CSR, consumer's trust on CSR and willingness to pay premium price with the purchase intention among generation Y in Malaysia based on below Table 4.8.

The result is tabulated in the Table 4.8 below for better understanding on the analytical result.

Table 4.8: The multiple regression analysis

Multiple Regression					
Multiple R	0.704				
R^2	0.495				
Adjusted R^2	0.491				
Standard Error	2.022				
		df	Analysis of Variance Sum of Square	Mean Square	P-value
Regression		3	1526.627	508.876	0.000
Residual		381	1557.436	4.088	
F=124.488			Significance of F=0.000		
Variable	b	Variable SE	Equation Beta (β)	T	Significance of t
Constant	5.199	0.832		6.249	0.0000

Consumers' awareness of CSR	0.007	0.068	0.004	0.105	0.9170
Consumers' trust of CSR	0.205	0.06	0.145	3.424	0.0010
Willingness to pay premium price	0.456	0.029	0.629	15.521	0.0000

From this above Table 4.8, it showed that the result obtained from multiple regression. R square is a statistical term that indicate how well the independent variables are in predicting and influencing the dependent variable. The higher the R square value will contribute to a better define in the predicting the dependent variable. In this study, the R square of the independent variable, purchase intention is 0.495, which signify that only 49.5% of the variation in purchase intention can be explained by the three independent variables, which are the consumers' awareness of CSR, consumers' trust in CSR and willingness to pay premium price. The balance of 50.5% of variation cannot be explained as it is beyond the scope of this study.

F-value represents a probability value that disclose the significant of the relationship between independent variables and dependent variables. It is used to determine whether the model has a statistically significant predictive capability. On the Table 4.8 as shown above, the value of significant F is 0.000 which is less than 0.05. Therefore, it is indicated that the purchase intention is significantly influence by consumers' awareness of CSR, consumers' trust in CSR and willingness to pay premium price.

Beta value is vital to measure how strongly each independent variable are in influencing the dependent variable. It can be served to reveal the actual influence of consumers' awareness of CSR, consumers' trust in CSR and willingness to pay premium price. If the beta value is high, it would signify a great impact of the independent variable over the dependent variable. From the Table 4.8, the beta value of the consumers' awareness of CSR is only 0.007 which giving a very minimal impact on the purchase intention. This might due to the generation Y has been living in the free flow of mass information since young. Thus, the CSR concept has been longed enough in the market that it is no longer impact on their purchase intention.

The beta value of consumers' trust in CSR is 0.205, while willingness to pay premium price is 0.456. Thus, it is indicating that the willingness to pay premium price will give a higher impact as independent variable on purchase intention, compared to the other two factors.

The multiple regression equation derived from above output is

Purchase Intention = 5.199 + 0.007 Consumers' awareness of CSR + 0.205 Consumers' trust in CSR+ 0.456 Willingness to pay premium price

From above equation, it shows that 1% increase in consumers' awareness of CSR will lead to 0.7% increase in purchase intention, with the condition that holding other variables constant. Next, the 1% increase in the consumers' trust in CSR will influence 20.5% of purchase intention, by assuming the other variables are kept constant. For the 1% increase in willingness to pay premium price will impact the raise in 45.6% of purchase intention provided all other variables are constant.

Thus, the result is able to accept the null hypothesis that there is significant relationship between consumers' awareness of CSR, consumers' trust in CSR and willingness to pay premium price with the purchase intention. Table 4.9 showed the summary of the hypotheses finding.

Table 4.9 Summary of hypotheses

Hypothesis	Findings
Hypothesis 1: There is a significant relationship between consumers' awareness of CSR and purchase intention among the generation Y in Malaysia.	Accepted
Hypothesis 2: There is a significant relationship between consumers' trust in CSR and purchase intention among the generation Y in Malaysia.	Accepted
Hypothesis 3: There is a significant relationship between the willingness to pay premium price and purchase intention among the generation Y in Malaysia.	Accepted

CHAPTER 5

Deliberation

The study is concluded with discussion and the recommendations suggested for future research. The overall summary of major findings in this study are first discussed in this chapter. Then, this section also has listed down the limitation of the study and lastly followed by a few appropriate suggestions for future study.

Discussion

This research is studied according to the research framework as discussed earlier. The research framework consists of three independent variables towards one dependent variable. This study is conducted to understand the impact of CSR on the purchase intention among generation Y in Malaysia to fill in the gaps that the particular focus group is studied locally due to the generation Y are the current and future work force in all the industry. Thus, the research questions, research objectives and hypotheses are developed. With that, the research are adopting the quantitative approach in the positivist paradigm in producing the statistical probable generalized results.

From this exploratory and cross-sectional study, the study has been adopting the convenience sampling method for data collection. There are 385 data collected from the google form surveyed through social media where most of the generation Y are actively engaged. In the data analysis section, the Cronbach alpha has been identified to be above 0.70 which indicated the data is relevant and consistent. Moreover, the preliminary analysis on the association of the three independent variables and the dependent variable are determined through Pearson's coefficient of correlation are done to confirm on the correlation.

By completing the multiple regression analysis, the objectives of this study are tested through the hypothesis as well as the behavioural responses of the Malaysian generation Y on the CSR. From the general objective in determining the relationship between consumers' awareness of CSR, consumers' trust in CSR and willingness to pay a premium price and purchase intention among the Malaysian generation Y, it can conclude that the relationship is significant particularly, each relationship is studied as below.

Objective 1

The objective 1 is to investigate the relationship between consumers' awareness of CSR and purchase intention among the generation Y in Malaysia. The result indicates that the hypothesis 1 is accepted as there is a positive relationship between consumers' awareness of CSR and purchase intention among the generation Y in Malaysia. This is concurrent with the research conducted by Lee & Shin (2009), Tian et al. (2011), Balcova (2012) and opposed the study conducted by Nasir et al. (2014).

The result also demonstrated that the relationship between the consumer's awareness of CSR and purchase intention is low compared to the other variables. In Table 4.8, the beta value is 0.007. This is relating to the demographic study of the Malaysian generation Y respondents in this survey. Firstly, most of the generation Y are well-educated. The statistic in Table 4.1 has shown majority (88%) are at least a degree holder. When they are being questioned on the familiarity on the concept of crporate social responsibility, this young group of consumers are also highly skew towards the scale of strongly agree which comprised of 24% neutral, 33% agree and 27% strongly agree.

Besides that, the survey questionnaire also covered on the target respondents' understanding about the issues addressed by Corporate Social Responsibility whereby most of the Malaysian generation Y are highly aware on the issues related to community involvement and development, environment, as well as human rights. Moreover, Malaysian generation Y are also generally knowing about CSR because there are 69% of the target respondents claimed themselves aware of any companies operating in Malaysia that can be considered socially responsible. Thus, when it comes to CSR, the Malaysian generation Y are concerned on this, in addition to the wide-spread of information through the social media and internet where most of the generation Y are very active in social media platform. Hence, they are no stranger to the concept of CSR where the free flow of information through the access of internet.

Aside of the CSR knowledge of the respondents, it also can be related to the income level of the respondents whereby it might be part of the factor in dictating them on their purchase intention. Although majority of the Malaysian generation Y are aware of CSR and pretty familiar with its concept, as well as able to point out the companies that practising CSR activities, like community involvement and development, but, their income level will hindrance on their purchase intention. From Table 4.8 shown that, majority of the generation Y is having the income level at below RM4000 which are mostly under B40 range. Hence, their spending power is restricted by their income and directly affecting on their purchase intention on the CSR products.

Perhaps, even after Malaysian generation Y are aware about CSR, they are still able to make a conscious purchase, or they might prefer to be conscious due to their income level at B40, therefore, the independent variable, the consumers' awareness of CSR is not that significant in making a great impact to their purchase intention. Hence, it also similar to the research conducted by Sen & Bhattacharya (2001) that the consumers' awareness of CSR will be low in affecting the consumers' ability to purchase. Moreover, it is also compliance to the concern on the CSR understanding are broad and defined widely. Hence, it is further determined that the complexity and dynamics of the CSR on purchase intention. Particularly, Malaysian generation Y are aware of CSR due to the exposure of information through social media, education or corporate CSR activities, but it would not be one of the significant factors to push them to purchase the CSR products.

Objective 2

The objective 2 is to examine the relationship between consumers' trust in CSR and purchase intention among the generation Y in Malaysia. The result indicated that the hypothesis 2 is accepted as there is a positive relationship between consumers' trust in CSR and purchase intention among the generation Y in Malaysia. The beta value obtained through the analysis is 0.205. This is similar to the findings from Du, Bhattacharya & Sen (2010), but the impact of consumers' trust in CSR might be as big as the willingness to pay premium price, which is comply to the condition as reported in the research of Balcova (2012) that this factor might have the least impact on the purchase intention. However, due to the difference in the cultural differences and languages variation, thus, the consumers' trust in CSR is not the least impact but intermediary, compared to the consumers' awareness of CSR and willingness to pay premium price. This finding also similar to the research done by Semuel and Chandra (2014) on Surabaya population.

To further discuss on the cultural differences and languages variation that cause the discrepancies on the study, the demographic characteristics of the target respondents, Malaysian generation Y are determined. From the result shown in Table 4.1, majority of the respondents are Malay and Chinese while India and other races are remained as minorities, which might reflect on the interest of the races towards the topic of this study. As trust are building through times, thus, it is harder to build and taking a much longer time to observe the effect on the purchase intention. As most of the Malaysian generation Y are aware of any companies operating in Malaysian are considered as socially responsible, thus, the familiarity of the companies' name and brand will give a stronger impact on purchase intention compared to the consumers' awareness. As such, the preliminary variable would be the awareness of the Malaysian generation Y and subsequently building their trust towards the CSR products, which able to give a higher impact on the purchase intention, compared to the consumers' awareness.

Next, the survey also identified that majority of the Malaysian generation Y are thinking that community involvement and development (74%), environment (69%) and human rights (65%) would be addressed by corporate social responsibility which have been conducted by the firms (Table 4.1). Thus, this might indicate that the firms could build a strong consumers' trust through these activities that could involve a large crowd as it compared to fair operating practices (40%) which is more focused on the firms' internal processes and hardly visible to the publics.

On the other hand, the gender ratio might be reflecting on this hypothesis, as there are higher number of female (62%) compared to male (38%) in answering this survey. It might indicate that there are more female respondents are interested to the topic of study as well as they are also sensitive to the purchase. For instance, the study by Cone Communications & Echo (2013) stated that female having a higher tendency towards CSR, would not really clear on the ultimate impact of CSR marketed by the company but will still trying out their best way to save the world whenever step into a store. Hence, it would be easier to build the consumers' trust in CSR of Malaysian generation Y female due to their initial interests as well as higher preference in shopping, compared to Malaysian generation Y male.

Hence, from the insights of this study, it is allowed us to understand that complexity of dynamics of CSR are closely related to the issues addressed by CSR, the gender as well as races which will impact on the level of the consumer's trust towards the firms as well as the CSR products. As such, the consumers' trust in CSR is important in affecting the purchase intention of Malaysian generation Y even this study do not show a high beta value in the analysis in Table 4.8 as consumers' trust are building over the time. Hence, the right activities like community involvement development, environmental and human rights CSR activities could be organized by the firms to build the consumers' trust as well as increase their favourable towards the brands and thus, increase the purchase intention on the CSR products.

Objective 3

The objective 3 is to investigate the relationship between consumers' awareness of CSR and purchase intention among the generation Y in Malaysia. Hypothesis 3 is accepted as there is a positive relationship between willingness to pay premium price and purchase intention among the generation Y in Malaysia. The beta value obtained from the multiple regression analysis in Table 4.8 has shown as 0.456, which indicated that for the 1% increase in willingness to pay premium price will raise 45.6% of purchase intention provided all other variables are constant. This result is consistent with the findings conducted by Dodd and Supa (2011). Thus, to raise the purchase intention of the generation Y, thus, have to increase their willingness to pay.

To raise their willingness, most firms should well inform their customers on the CSR activities, as per reported by Loureiro & Lotade (2005) and Govindasamy, DeCongelio and Bhuyan (2006). This is also suggested to invest the resources in developing CSR activities like community involvement and development, environment and human rights which are deemed to be the highest vote among the other CSR issues, as these are the activities that being known by the Malaysian generation Y as shown in Table 4.1. It is deduced that Malaysian generation Y are more familiar with the concept of CSR through the define of these listed activities, and thus able to give a better approach to reach to the customers on CSR products which later convert to the increase of the consumers' purchase intention.

It is also vital to highlight on the income level of the Malaysian generation Y from Table 4.1. According to the Department of Statistic Malaysia, the median household income of T20 is at least RM13,148, while M40 is at RM6,275 while B40 is RM3,000. Although most of the Malaysian generation Y are well-educated but their salary level might not parallel to their income. Thus, majority (56%) of the Malaysian generation Y are earning in the range of B40 and a few of them (4%) are earning in the range of M40.

Therefore, different salary range to them will have a different range of disposable income to these young consumers. With that, the independent variable of willingness to pay premium price would certainly affecting their purchase intention with the minimum disposable income earned, particularly for the Malaysian generation Y that are in B40 group. Thus, there is a stronger relationship at beta value of 0.456 between willingness to pay premium price and the purchase intention, compared to the relationship of the other two independent variables, which are the consumers' awareness (beta value of 0.007) and trust (beta value of 0.205) in CSR with the purchase intention.

All the independent variables are having a positive association with the purchase intention of generation Y in Malaysia. However, the consumers' awareness of CSR does not give a big impact to them which might due to the well-spread of CSR information across the countries. This also due to the behavioural of the country as in Malaysia has a high collectivism that could spread the news faster to the closer one. Furthermore, for the consumer's trust of CSR is similar to the findings in Surabaya which might implies that the generation Y in the close-related region might portray similar pattern. Nevertheless, consumers' trust in CSR are still impacting moderately towards purchase intention. Thus, to increase the consumers' purchase intention, the business can focus on building the consumers' trust in CSR.

Lastly, the willingness to pay premium price is impacting the purchase intention of generation Y greatly due to the newly joined workforce or young working adults are price sensitive. Thus, if they are convinced for the benefits received from the premium price set, they are good to purchase such products as part of CSR. Hence, this study is crucial for the management to look at these independent variables and focus on developing the right strategy to build the consumers' trust and increase their willingness to pay the premium price.

Contribution

From this study, it able to provide a foundation of knowledge on the purchase intention of generation Y in Malaysia, as such the factors like consumers' awareness of CSR, consumers' trust in CSR and willingness to pay premium prices are studied. Thus, the research is used to extend the knowledge of how a company put its strategy especially CSR advertising as its promotional mix to influence customer purchase intention. Next, the research is useful in developing marketing strategy to improve relationship marketing towards customer. This research may also be used as a base for future academic research on generation Y towards CSR as well as their purchase intention.

Limitations

There are a few limitations throughout the entire of this study due to its exploratory nature and the adoption of convenient sampling method.

First, not every factor, such as the perceived CSR, CSR brand reputation, consumers' perception of a CSR corporation's reputation and activities, that affects the purchase intention of generation Y in Malaysia are throughout studied in this study. Indeed, this study is only able to include three variables such as consumers' awareness of CSR, consumers' trust in CSR and willingness to pay premium price in determining the purchase intention of generation Y in Malaysia. A bias result may be produced due to any omitted variables that not being included in this study which could have some impacts on the purchase intention of generation Y in Malaysia.

Next, the data collected for this study is only 385 which might only comprise a small population of generation Y in Malaysia. Even though according to the research conducted by Taherdoost (2017), the representative sampling size for more than 1,000,000 people of population, the samples size should be at least 384 to achieve the confident level of 95%; but there might be biasness in sampling error from the respondents.

Lastly, the Likert scale question adopted in the survey method are scaled from 1 to 5 which some respondents would tend to choose the option 3 as in neutral towards the questions asked as they might not fully understand the questions or just prefer to complete the questionnaires quickly. Hence, it might not able to generate a more representative data for such neutral responses.

Recommendations for Future Research

There are several recommendations for the future research due to the limitations that encountered in this research. It is necessary to find a way to reduce or eliminate those limitations in order to obtain a result with higher consistency and reliability for this research.

For further in-depth study, it is recommended to include more independent variables that impacting the purchase intention of generation Y in Malaysia. More variables will provide a better insight in understanding each variable assessed in this research. Future research also may use probability sampling to generalize the result or use quota sampling of gender, age, or income level to know how each category view on the topic. Furthermore, the future research should allow the diverse participation of respondents not only from consumers point of view but also from the stakeholders and employee on the CSR topics. Another variable which will affect the purchase intention, such the CSR brand reputation should be examined further.

The next recommendation for future research would be the types of questions in the questionnaires. The options for the Likert scale questions should revised to be in even instead of odd number so that the respondents would be able to provide a more certain response for a question instead of given neutral responses which basically not useful in generate a representative result. Nevertheless, it would lead to another disadvantage which is forced choice question. Thus, another data collection method should be executed in order to generate a better response for the study such as interview the customers in Malaysia. By doing this, it can generate a deeper understanding on how the independent variables, such the brand reputation, CSR activities are impacting on the purchase intention of the generation Y in Malaysia. This is a qualitative method which is very useful since some of the questions in the questionnaire are very subjective where only face interview could reduce the ambiguous of the question.

CONCLUSION

In a nutshell, most of the Malaysian generation Y are highly aware on the issues related to community involvement and development, environment, as well as human rights and dynamics of the CSR on purchase intention among them. Further, the awareness of the Malaysian generation Y and subsequently building their trust towards the CSR products, which able to give a higher impact on the purchase intention, compared to the consumers' awareness. They are willingness to pay premium price would certainly affecting their purchase intention with the minimum disposable income earned, though they are in B40 group category.

REFERENCES

Aaker, D. A. (1996). Measuring brand equity across products and markets. *California Management Review, 38* (3), pp. 102-120. http://dx.doi.org/10.2307/41165845

Abdul, M.Z. & Ibrahim, S. (2002). Executive and management attitudes towards corporate social responsibility in Malaysia. *Corporate Governance, 2* (4), pp.10-16.

Abram, S., Luther, J. (2004) Born with the chip. *Library Journal, 129*(8), pp. 34-37.

Aguilar, F. X., & Vlosky, R. P. (2007). Consumer willingness to pay price premiums for environmentally certified wood products in the US. *Forest Policy and Economics, 9*(8), pp.1100–1112.

Alch, M.L. (2000) The echo-boom generation: a growing force in American society. *The Futurist, 34*(5), pp. 42 – 46.

Alniacik, U., Alniacik, E., Genc, N. (2010). How corporate social responsibility information influences stakeholders' intentions. *Corporate Social Responsibility and Environmental Mangement, 18* (4), pp. 308-323.

Altman, W. (2007). Working for the greater good? *Engineering Management*. Retrieved 27 July 2010, from www.theiet.org/management

Ang, S. H. (2000). The power of money: A cross-cultural analysis of business-related beliefs. *Journal of World Business*, 35(1), pp.43–60.

Anselmsson, J. and Johansson, U. (2007). Corporate social responsibility and the positioning of grocery brands: an exploratory study of retailer and manufacturer brands at point of purchase. *International Journal of Retail & Distribution Management*, 35(10), pp.835-856.

Anselmsson, J., Johansson, U. and Persson, N. (2007). Understanding price premium for grocery products: a conceptual model of customer-based brand equity. *Journal of Product & Brand Management*, 16(6), pp.401-414.

Arora, N. & Henderson, T. (2007). Embedded Premium Promotion: Why It Works and How to Make It More Effective. *Marketing Science*, 26(4), 514-531. https://doi.org/10.1287/mksc.1060.0247

Autio, M., & Wilska, T. A. (2005). Young people in knowledge society: possibilities to fulfil ecological goals. *Progress in industrial ecology, an international journal*, 2(3), pp. 403-426

Bargiela, A., Nakashima, T., Pedrycz, W. (2005). Iterative gradient descent approach to multiple regression with fuzzy data, paper presented to conference: Fuzzy information processing society, 2005 (NAFIPS 2005), North America, 2005. Viewed 7th September 2018.

Beckmann, S. C. (2007). Consumers and corporate social responsibility: Matching the unmatchable? *Australasian Marketing Journal (AMJ)*, 15(1), pp. 27-36.

Belk, R. W., Devinney, T., & Eckhardt, G. (2005). Consumer ethics across cultures. *Consumption Markets & Culture*, 8(3), pp. 275-289.

Bhattacharya, C., & Sen, S. (2004). Doing better at doing good: When, why, and how consumers respond to corporate social initiatives. *California Management Review*, 47(1), pp. 9-24.

Bickman, L., & Rog, D. J. (Eds.). (2008). *The Sage handbook of applied social research methods*. Sage publications.

Bilikova, N. (2015). *Consumers' perceptions of corporate social responsibility in Czech Republic*. Unpublished master's thesis. University of Huddersfield, Czech Republic.

Black, A. (2010). Gen Y: Who they are and how they learn. Retrieved from https://files.eric.ed.gov/fulltext/EJ872487.pdf

Blackwell, R., Miniard, P., & Engel, J. (2006). *Consumer Behaviour*. Mason, Ohio: Thomson/South-Western.

Bohrnstedt, G.W., Knoke, D. (1994). *Statistics for Social Data Analysis*. Itasca, IL: F. E. Peacock Publishers.

Bolton, L. E., Warlop, L. &, J.W. (2003). Explorations in Price (Un)Fairness. *Journal of Consumer Research*, 29, pp.474–491.

Boonpattarakan, A. (2012). An experimental design to test the main and interaction effects of CSR involvement, brand naming and pricing on purchase intentions in Thailand. *International Journal of Business and Management*, 7(16), pp. 62-79. http://dx.doi.org/10.5539/ijbm.v7n16p62

Bowen H. R. (1953). Social Responsibilities of the Businessman, N.Y.: Harper &

Brosdahl, D. J., & Carpenter, J. M. (2011), "Shopping orientations of US males: A generational cohort comparison", *Journal of Retailing and Consumer Services*, 18, pp. 548-554.

Brown, T. J., & Dacin, P. A. (1997). The company and the product: Corporate associations and consumer product responses. *Journal of Marketing*, 61(1), pp.68-84.

Bryman, A. and Bell, E., (2007). *Business Research Methods*. 2ed. Great Clarendon: Oxford University Press.

Carroll, A.B. (1979). A three-dimensional Conceptual Model of Corporate Performance. *Academy of Management Review*, 4 (4), pp. 497-505.

Carroll, A.B. (1991). The Pyramid of Corporate Social Responsibility: Toward the Moral Management of Organizational Stakeholders. *Business Horizons*, 34 (4), 39-48.

Carvalho, S. W., Sen, S. Mota, M.d.O., Lima, R.C.d. (2010). Consumer Reactions to CSR: A Brazilian perspective. *Journal of Business Ethics*, 91(2), pp.291-310.

Castaldo, S., Perrini, F., Misani, N., & Tencati, A. (2009). The missing link between corporate social responsibility and consumer trust: The case of fair-trade products. *Journal of Business Ethics*, 84 (1), pp. 1-15. http://dx.doi.org/10.1007/s10551-008-9669-4

Chapple, W., & Moon, J. (2005). Corporate social responsibility (CSR) in Asia: A seven-country study of CSR website reporting. *Business and Society*, 44(4), pp.415–441.

Chaudhuri, A., & Holbrook, M. B. (2001). The chain of effects from brand trust and brand affect to brand performance: The role of brand loyalty. *Journal of Marketing*, 65(2), pp.81–93.

Chladek, A., Florack, A. & Kleber, J. (2013). The Moderating Role of Numeracy in the Effectiveness of Cause-Related Marketing. En *Advances in Consumer Research (41)*, eds. Botti, S. y Labroo, A. Duluth, Minesota: Association for Consumer Research.

Cone Communications & Echo. (2013). *Global CSR Study.* Boston: Cone Communications & Echo. Retrieved 2015-04-14, from http://www.conecomm.com/global-csr-study/

Crawford, F. & Mathews, R. (2001). *The myth of excellence: Why great companies never try to be the best at everything.* New York, NY: Crown Business.

Creusen, M.E.H., Hultink, E.J., Eling, K. (2013). Choice of consumer research methods in the front end of new product development. *International Journal of Market Research,* 55(1), pp.81-104.

Crowther, D. (2003). Corporate Social Reporting: Genuine Action or Window Dressing? In D. Crowther, L. Rayman-Bacchus (Eds) *Perspectives on Corporate Social Responsibility* (pp.140-160). UK: Ashgate: Aldershot.

Darus, F. (2012). Embracing corporate social responsibility in Malaysia-Towards

De Pelsmacker, P., Driesen, L., & Rayp, G. (2006). Do consumers care about ethics? Willingness to pay for fair-trade coffee. *Journal of Consumer Affairs,* 39(2), pp.363–385.

Deegan, C. & Unerman, J. (2011). *Financial Accounting Theory.* (2. European ed.) Maidenhead: Mc Graw-Hill Education.

Deegan, C., 2002. Introduction: The legitimising effect of social and environmental disclosures-a theoretical foundation. *Accounting, Auditing and Accountability Journal,* 15 (3), pp.282-311.

Department of Statistic Malaysia, 2018. The Population by age in Malaysia.

Djamasbi, S., Tullis, T., Siegel, M., Capozzo, D., Groezinger, R., & Ng, F. (2008). Generation Y & web design: Usability through eye tracking. *AMCIS 2008 Proceedings,* pp.77.

Dodd, Melissa D & Supa W., (2011). Understanding the Effect of Corporate Social Responsibility on Consumer Purchase Intention. *Public Relations Journal*, 5(3), pp.1-19.

Du, S., Bhattacharya, C. B., and Sen, S. (2007). Reaping relational rewards from corporate social responsibility: The role of competitive positioning. International *Journal of Research in Marketing*, 24(3), pp. 224-241.

Easterby-Smith, M., Thorpe, R. & Lowe, A. (2002). *Management Research: An Introduction.* 2nd edition. London: Sage Publications

Ekström K. M., Hjelmgren D. & Salomonson N. (2015). Environmental consumer socialization among Generation Swing and Y: a study of clothing consumption. In Ekström K.M. (Eds.), *Waste management and sustainable consumption: reflections on consumer waste.* New York: Routledge.

Edelman. (2014). *Brand purpose look ahead: Power of participation platforms.* Accesado el 16 de diciembre de 2015. Disponible en http://purpose.edelman.com/2014-brand-purpose-look-ahead-power-of-participation-platforms/

Erdem, T. and Swait, J. (2004). Brand Credibility, Brand Consideration, and Choice. *Journal of Consumer Research*, 31(1), pp.191-198.

Esch, F., Langner, T. B., Schmitt, H., & Geus, P. (2006). Are brands forever? How brand knowledge and relationships affect current and future purchases. *The Journal of Product and Brand Management*, 15 (2), pp. 98-105. http://dx.doi.org/10.1108/10610420610658938

Espejel, J., Fandos, C. and Flavián, C. (2008). Consumer satisfaction. *British Food Journal*, 110(9), pp.865-881.

Fandos, C.H, Flavian, C. Intrinsic and extrincis quality attributes, loyalty and buying intention: An analysis for a PDO product. *British Food Journal, 108*(8), pp. 642-662.

Farris, R., Chong, F., & Dunning, D. (2002). Generation Y: Purchasing power and implications for marketing. *Academy of Marketing Studies Journal, 6* (2), pp.89-101.

Fatma, M., & Rahman, Z. (2016). The CSR's influence on customer responses in Indian banking sector. *Journal of Retailing and Consumer Services, 29*, pp.49-57. http://doi.org/10.1016/j.jretconser.2015.11.008

Field, A. (2000). Discovering statistics using SPSS for Windows, [online]. Retrieved from http://books.google.sk/books?id=e9RidWtoVTQC&printsec=frontcover&dq=statistics+SPSS&source=bl&ots=es_bHLeCAx&sig=Ep_PkXB9wRViRMR5B5f9aiaCp5w&hl=en&sa=X&ei=Ve1uULjjEvLR4QSFl4CACg&redir_esc=#v=onepage&q=statistics%20SPSS&f=false [Accessed 17 March 2019].

Fisher, B., Turner, R. K., & Morling, P. (2009). Defining and classifying ecosystem services for decision making. *Ecological Economics, 68*(3), pp.643–653.

Foscht, T., Schloffer, J., Maloles III, C., & Chia, S. L. (2009). Assessing the outcomes of Generation-Y customers' loyalty. *International Journal of Bank marketing, 27*(3), pp.218-241.

Friestad, M., Wright, P. (1994). Persuasion knowledge model: how people cope with persuasion attempts. *Journal of Consumer Research, 21*(1), pp. 1 – 31.

Garcia-Conde, M.G., Marin, L., Maya, S.R. (2016). The role of generativity in the effects of corporate social responsibility on consumer behaviour. *Sustainability, 8*, pp.1-14.

Geokhaji, E., Landstrom, A. (2015). *The influence of CSR on Millennials' buying behaviour: A case study of Swedish University students.* Unpublished degree thesis. Lulea University of Technology, Sweden.

George, D., & Mallery, M. (2010). *SPSS for Windows Step by Step: A Simple Guide and Reference, 17.0 update* (10a ed.) Boston: Pearson.

Geraci, J.C., Nagy, J. (2004) Millennials – the new media generation. *Young Consumers: Insight and Ideas for Responsible Marketers,* 5(2), pp.17 – 24.

Goi, C.L. & Yong, K.H. (2009). Contribution of public relations (PR) to corporate social responsibility (CSR): A review on Malaysia perspective. *International Journal of Marketing Studies, 1* (2), pp.46-49.

Googins, B.K., Mirvis, P.H., & Rochlin, S.A. (2007). *Beyond good company: Next generation corporate citizenship.* New York, NY: Palgrave Macmillan.

Govindasamy, R., DeCongelio, M., & Bhuyan, S. (2006). An evaluation of consumer willingness to pay for organic produce in the Northeastern US. *Journal of Food Products Marketing, 11*(4), pp.3–20.

Goyal, R. (2014). *A study on purchase Intentions of consumers towards selected luxury fashion products with special reference to Pune region.* Unpublished master thesis. Dypatil University. Mumbai.

Habel, J., Schons, L. M., Alavi, S. & Wieseke, J. (2016), Warm Glow or Extra Charge? The Ambivalent Effect of Corporate Social Responsibility Activities on Customers' Perceived Price Fairness. *Journal of Marketing,* 80 (1), 84-105. https://doi.org/10.1509/jm.14.0389

Hair, J. F., Black, W. C., Babin, B. J., & Anderson, R. E. (2010). *Multivariate Data Analysis* (7th ed.). Upper Saddle River, NJ: Prentice Hall.

Halim, W, Z, W., Hamed, A, B., (2005). Consumer purchase Intention at traditional restaurant and fast food restaurant. *ANZMAC 2005 Conference: Consumer Behavior.*

Heaney, J-G., Gleeson, D. (2008). Corporate social responsibility in business courses: how can generation Y learn? *Academy of World Business, Marketing & Management Development Conference*, Rio de Janeiro, Brazil July 14-17.

Henrie, K.M. & Taylor, D.C. (2009). Use of persuasion knowledge by the millennial generation. *Young Consumers: Insight and Ideas for Responsible Marketers*, 10(1), pp.71-81.

Hopkins, M. (2003). The business case for CSR: Where are we? *International Journal of Business Performance Management*, 5(2/3), pp.125-140. http://dx.doi.org/10.1504/IJBPM.2003.003261

Howe, N., Strauss, W. (2000) *Millennials Rising: The Next Great Generation.* New York: Vintage Books.

Hwang, C.G., Lee, Y.A., Diddi, S. (2013). Generation Y's purchase intentions with organic, fair trade, and recycled apparel and their relationships to moral obligation. Proceedings of *International Textile and Apparel Association.* New Orleans, Louisiana.

Introduction to SAS. UCLA: Statistical Consulting Group. Retrieved from https://stats.idre.ucla.edu/sas/modules/sas-learning-moduleintroduction-to-the-features-of-sas/ (assessed on 20th March 2019).

Jun Yu & Renate Meyer (2006). Multivariate Stochastic Volatility Models: Bayesian Estimation and Model Comparison. *Econometric Reviews*, 25(2-3), pp.361-384.

Kaya, G., Otken, A. B., Okan, E. Y. (2014). Turkish students' perceptions of social responsibility and voluntarism. *9th MIBES International Conference*. pp. 27-38.

Keegan, W.J. & Green, M.C. (2013). *Global marketing*. (7. ed.) Boston, MA: Pearson.

Keh, H. T., & Xie, Y. (2009). Corporate reputation and customer behavioral intentions: The roles of trust, identification and commitment. *Industrial Marketing Management*, 38(7), pp. 732-752.

Kent State University Libraries. (2017, May 15). *SPSS tutorials: Independent samples t test*. Retrieved May 17, 2017, from http://libguides.library.kent.edu/SPSS/IndependentTTest

Kilian, T. & Hennigs, N. (2014). Corporate social responsibility and environmental reporting in controversial industries. *European Business Review*, 26(1), pp.79-101.

Kimber, D., & Lipton, P. (2005). Corporate governance and business ethics in the Asia-Pacific region. *Business and Society*, 44(2), pp.178–210.

Ko, E., Taylor, C.R., Wagner, U., Ji, H. (2008). Relationship among CEO image, corporate image and employment brand value in fashion industry. *Journal of Global Academy of Marketing Science*, 18(4), pp.311-331.

Krämer W. (2011) Durbin–Watson Test. In: Lovric M. (eds) International Encyclopaedia of Statistical Science. Springer, Berlin, Heidelberg

Lee, J., & Lee, Y. (2015). The interactions of CSR, self-congruity and purchase intention among Chinese consumers. *Australasian Marketing Journal*, 23 (1), pp.19-26. http://doi.org/10.1016/j.ausmj.2015.01.003

Lee, J.S., Han, H., Hsu, L.T., Kim, Y. (2010). Understanding how consumers view green hotels: How a hotel's green image can influence behavioural intentions. *Journal of Sustainable Tourism*, 18(7), pp.901-914.

Lee, K. H., & Shin, D. (2010). Consumers' responses to CSR activities: The linkage between increased awareness and purchase intention. Public Relations Review, 36 (2), pp.193-195. http://doi.org/10.1016/j.pubrev.2009.10.014

Lingreen, A., Swaen, V., Johnston, W. (2009). The supporting function of marketing in corporate social responsibility. *Corporate Reputation Review*, 12(2), pp. 120-139.

Loureiro, M. L., & Lotade, J. (2005). Do fair trade and eco-labels in coffee wake up the consumer conscience? *Ecological Economics*, 53(1), pp.129–138.

Low, C. K. (2004). A road map for corporate governance in East Asia. *North-western Journal of International Law and Business*, 25, pp.165–203.

Lu, J.Y. and P. Castka, 2009. Corporate Social Responsibility in Malaysia-Experts' Views and Perspectives. *Corporate Social Responsibility and Environmental Management*, 16 (3), pp.146-154.

Malhotra, N. K. (2007). *Marketing research: An applied orientation*. Upper Saddle River, NJ: Pearson/Prentice Hall.

Maignan, I. (2001). Consumers' perceptions of corporate social responsibilities: A cross-cultural comparison. *Journal of business ethics*, 30(1), pp. 57-72.

Maignan, I., & Ralston, D. A. (2002). Corporate social responsibility in Europe and the US: Insights from businesses' self-presentations. *Journal of International Business Studies*, 33(3), pp.497–514.

Malaysia Population by age. (2018). Retrieved from http://pqi.stats.gov.my/result.php?token=ebf358fbacc579cfbbb50395dad74a3

Mamun, M.A., Shaikh, J.M., Easmin, R. (2017). Corporate social responsibility disclosure in Malaysia business. *Academy of Strategic Management Journal*, 16(2), pp.29-47.

Margolis, J. D., Elfenbein, H. A., & Walsh, J. P. (2007). Does it pay to be good? A meta-analysis and redirection of research on the relationship between corporate social and financial performance. Ann Arbor, 1001, 48109-1234.

McCasland, M. (2005). Mobile marketing to Millennials. *Young Consumers: Insight and Ideas for Responsible Marketers*, 6(3), pp.8 – 13.

McCrindle, M. (2008). Bridging the gap: an employer guide to managing and retaining the new generation of apprentices and trainees. The ABC of XYZ.

Mendenhall, W., Sincich, T. (1989). *A second course in business statistics: Regression analysis*. US: Macmillan Pub Co.

Mohr, L. A., & Webb, D. J. (2005). The effects of corporate social responsibility and price on consumer responses. *Journal of Consumer Affairs*, 39(1), pp.121-147.

Mohr, L. A., Webb, D. J., & Harris, K. E. (2001). Do consumers expect companies to be socially responsible? The impact of corporate social responsibility on buying behavior. *Journal of Consumer affairs*, 35(1), pp.45-72.

Mollen, A., & Wilson, M. (2010). Engagement, telepresence and interactivity in online consumer experience: Reconciling scholastic and managerial perspectives. *Journal of Business Research*, 63 (9/10), pp.919-925. http://dx.doi.org/10.1016/j.jbusres.2009.05.01

Morton, L. P. (2002). Targeting generation Y. *Public Relations Quarterly*, 47(2), pp.46–48.

Morwitz, V. G. & Schmittlein, D. (1992). Using segmentation to improve sales forecasts based on purchase intent: Which intenders actually buy? *Journal of Marketing Research, 29,* pp.391-405.

Morwitz, V. G., Steckel, J. & Gupta, A. (1996). *When do purchase intentions predict sales?* Working Paper, Stern School of Business, New York University, NY

Mulaessa, N., and Wang, H. (2017). The effect of corporate social responsibility (CSR) activities on consumers purchase intention in China: Mediating role of consumer support for responsible business. *International Journal of Marketing Studies, 9(1),* pp.73-81.

Nasir, N.E.M., Halim, N.A.A., Sallem, N.R.M., Jasni, N.S., Aziz, N.F. (2014). Corporate Social Responsibility: An Overview from Malaysia. J. *Appl. Environ. Biol. Sd., 4(10S),* pp.82-87.

N.D. (May 6, 2018). Redesigning Malaysia's Higher Education System. Star. Retrieved from https://www.thestar.com.my/news/education/2018/05/06/redesigning-malaysias-higher-education-system/

Neuborne, E., Kerwin, K. (1999) Generation Y. *Business Week,* 15th February, No. 3616.

Newell, S. and Goldsmith, R. (2001). The development of a scale to measure perceived corporate credibility. *Journal of Business Research, 52(3),* pp.235-247.

Ng, E. S. W., Schwitzer, L. & Lyons, S. (2010) New generation, great expectations: a field study of the Millennial generation. *Journal of Business and Psychology, 25(2),* pp.281 – 292.

Ng, E. S., Schweitzer, L., & Lyons, S. T. (2010). New generation, great expectations: A field study of the millennial generation. *Journal of Business and Psychology, 25(2),* pp.281-292.

Nunnally, J. C. (1978). *Psychometric theory* (2nd ed.). New York: McGraw-Hill.

Öberseder, M., Schlegelmilch, B. B., & Murphy, P. E. (2013). CSR practices and consumer perceptions. *Journal of Business Research*, 66(10), pp.1839-1851.

Paço, A.D., Alves, H., Shiel, C., & Filho, W. L. (2013). A multi-country level analysis of the environmental attitudes and behaviors among young consumers. *Journal of Environmental Planning and Management*, 56(10), pp.1532-1548.

Parsa, H. G., Lord, K. R., Putrevu, S., & Kreeger, J. (2015). Corporate social and environmental responsibility in services: Will consumers pay for it? *Journal of Retailing and Consumer Services*, 22, pp.250-260. http://doi.org/10.1016/j.jretconser.2014.08.006

Paul, P. (2001) Getting inside Gen Y. *American Demographics*, 23(9), pp. 42 – 49.

Pérez, A. and Rodríguez del Bosque, I. (2013). Measuring CSR Image: Three Studies to Develop and to Validate a Reliable Measurement Tool. *Journal of Business Ethics*, 118(2), pp.265-286.

Pirsch, J., Gupta, S., & Grau, S. L. (2007). A framework for understanding corporate social responsibility programs as a continuum: An exploratory study. *Journal of Business Ethics*, 70, pp.125–140.

Pivato, S., Misani, N., & Tencati, A. (2008). The impact of corporate social responsibility on consumer trust: The case of organic food. *Business Ethics: A European Review*, 17(1), pp.3–12.

Pomering, A. and Dolnicar, S. (2009). Assessing the Prerequisite of Successful CSR Implementation: Are Consumers Aware of CSR Initiatives? *Journal of Business Ethics*, 85(S2), pp.285-301.

Porter, M.E & Kramer, M. R. (2006). The corporate advantage of corporate philanthropy. *Harvard Business Review, 86,* pp.57-68.

Porter, M.E. & Kramer, M.R. (2006). Strategy and society. The link between Competitive advantage and corporate social responsibility. *Harvard Business Review,12,* pp.78-92.

Rahim, A.R., Jalaludin, F.W, Tajuddin, K. (2011). The importance of corporate social responsibility on consumer behaviour in Malaysia. *Asian Academy of Management Journal, 16*(1), pp.119-139.

Ramasamy, B. & Ting H.W. (2004). A comparative analysis of corporate social responsibility awareness: Malaysian and Singaporean firms. *Journal of Corporate Citizenship, 13,* pp.109-123.

Ramasamy, B., & Yeung, M. (2009). Chinese consumers' perception of corporate social responsibility (CSR). *Journal of Business Ethics, 88*(SUPPL. 1), pp.119-132. http://doi.org/10.1007/s10551-008-9825-x

Ray, C. C. (2008). A Cross-Cultural Comparison of Corporate Social Responsibility Practices: America and China. *Master's Thesis,* University of Tennessee.

Salmones, M., Crespo, A. and Bosque, I. (2005). Influence of Corporate Social Responsibility on Loyalty and Valuation of Services. *Journal of Business Ethics, 61*(4), pp.369-385.

Saunders, M., Lewis, P. & Thornhill, A. (2009). *Research methods for business students.* 5th edition. Essex: Pearson Education Limited.

Saunders, M., Lewis, P., & Thornhill, A. (2012). *Research methods for business students* (6th; 6. ed.). Harlow: Pearson.

Schneider, A., Hommel, G., & Blettner, M. (2010). Linear regression analysis: part 14 of a series on evaluation of scientific publications. *Deutsches Arzteblatt International,* 107(44), 776-82.

Semuel, H. & Chandra, S.S. (2014). The analysis of corporate social responsibility implementation effects towards price fairness, trust and purchase intention at Oriflame cosmetics products in Surabaya. *Procedia-Social and Behavioural Sciences,* 155, pp. 42-47.

Sen, S., & Bhattacharya, C. B. (2001). Does Doing Good Always Lead to Doing Better? Consumer Reactions to Corporate Social Responsibility. *Journal of Marketing Research,* 38 (2), pp. 225-243.

Sen, S., Bhattacharya, C. B., & Korschun, D. (2006). The role of corporate social responsibility in strengthening multiple stakeholder relationships: A field experiment. *Journal of the Academy of Marketing science,* 34(2), pp.158-166.

Sharma, S. K., & Mehta, S. (2012). Where Do We Go from Here? Viewing Corporate Social Responsibility through a sustainability lens. *Journal of Contemporary Management Research,* 6(2), pp.69-76.

Sillman, A., McCaffrey, C.R., Peterson, E.R. (2018). Where are the global Millennials? *Global Business Policy Council.* Retrieved from https://www.atkearney.com/web/global-business-policy-council/article?/a/where-are-the-gslobal-millennials-

Smith, R.E. (2011). Defining corporate social responsibility: A systems approach for socially responsible capitalism. *Master of Philosophy Theses 9.* Retrieved from http://repository.upenn.edu/od_theses_mp/9

Sobczak, A., Debucquet, G. & Havard, Ch. (2006) The impact of higher education on students' and young managers' perception of companies and CSR: an exploratory analysis. *Corporate governance*, 6(4), pp. 463 – 474.

Sullivan, P., & Heitmeyer, J. (2008). Looking at Gen Y shopping preferences and intentions: exploring the role of experience and apparel involvement. *International Journal of Consumer Studies*, 32(3), pp.285-295.

Susniene, D., Sargunas, G. (2009). Prerequisites of stakeholder management in an organization. *Inzinerine Ekonomika-Engineering Economics*, 2(62), pp.58-64.

sustaining value creation. *Malaysian Accounting Review, Special issue*, 11 (2), pp. 1-13.

Swaen, V., Chumpitaz, R. C. (2008). Impact of Corporate Social Responsibility on Consumer Trust. *Recherche et Applications en Marketing*, 23(4), pp. 7-33.

Syrett, M., Lammiman, J. (2004). Advertising and millennials. *Young Consumers: Insight and Ideas for Responsible Marketers*, 5(4), pp.62 – 73.

Taherdoost, H. (2017). Determining sample size; how to calculate survey sample size. *International Journal of Economics and Management Systems*, 2, pp.237-239.

Talbott, S. L. (2012). Generation Y and Sustainability. Unpublished thesis. University of Tennessee: Tenessee.

Thomas, A.B. (2004). *Research skills for management studies*. London: Routledge.

Tian, Z., Wang, R., & Wen, Y. (2011). Consumer responses to corporate social responsibility (CSR) in China. *Journal of Business Ethics*, 101(2), pp.197-212.

Trapero, F.G.A., Lozada, V.D.C.M.D. & Garcia, J.D.L.G. (2010). Consumers and their buying decision making based on price and information about corporate social responsibility (CSR). Case Study: Undergraduate students from a private university in Mexico. *Estudios Gerenciales*,26 (107), pp. 103-117.

Tsoutsoura, M. (2004). Corporate social responsibility and financial performance. Center for Responsible Business.

Vaaland, T. I., Heide, M., & Grønhaug, K. (2008). Corporate social responsibility: investigating theory and research in the marketing context. *European Journal of Marketing*, 42 (9/10), pp.927-953. http://doi.org/10.1108/03090560810891082

Varadarajan, P. R., & Menon, A. (1988). Cause-related marketing: A coalignment of marketing strategy and corporate philanthropy. *American Marketing*

Voon, J.P., Ngui, K.S., Agrawal, A. (2011). Determinants of Willingness to Purchase Organic Food: An Exploratory Study using Structural Equation Modeling. *International Food and Agribusiness Management Review*, 14 (2), pp. 103-120.

Walliser, G.B., Scott, I. (2018). Redefining corporate social responsibility in an era of globalization and regulatory hardening. *American Business Law Journal*, 55 (1).

Welford, R. J. (2004). Corporate social responsibility in Europe and Asia: Critical elements and best practice. *Journal of Corporate Citizenship*, 13, pp.31–47.

Welford, R. J. (2005). Corporate social responsibility in Europe, North America and Asia: 2004 survey results. *Journal of Corporate Citizenship*, 17, pp.33–52

Westwood, R. I., & Posner, B. Z. (1997). Managerial values across cultures: Australia, Hong Kong and the United States. *Asia Pacific Journal of Management*, 14(1), pp.31–66.

Xia, L., Monroe, K.B. & Cox J.L. (2004). The Price is Unfair! A Conceptual Framework of Price Fairness Perceptions. *Journal of Marketing* 68(4), pp.1–15.

Zia, N.U., Sohail, M. (2016). How Customers are willingto pay price premium on the bases of brand image for food brands? *Arabina Journal of Business and Management Review,* 5(12).

APPENDIX

Dear Sir/Madam,

I am a Master student from Putra Business School, currently conducting a master research on "The Impact of Corporate Social Responsibility on the Purchase Intention amongst Generation Y in Malaysia". The purpose of this study is to study the relationship between Corporate Social Responsibility (CSR) and Purchase Intention among Generation Y in Malaysia.

Kindly complete this questionnaire as your honest responses would be highly appreciated. There are no right or wrong answers to the questions. All information provided is purely for academic purposes and will be kept anonymous and confidential at all times.

Thanking you in advance for your participation in this survey.

Part I

Please tick [√] in the appropriate box that best describe your personal characteristics.

Gender :	[ ]	[ ] Female	
Age :	[ ] 21-25	[ ] 26-30	[ ] 31-35
Ethnicity :	[ ] Malay		
	[ ] Chinese		
	[ ] India		
	[ ] Others		
Education level :	[ ] SPM	[ ] A-level/ STPM/ Pra-U	[ ] Diploma
	[ ] Undergraduate	[ ] Postgraduate	[ ] PhD

5. Income level : [ ] Below RM1000
   [ ] RM1001-2000
   [ ] RM2001-3000
   [ ] RM3001-4000
   [ ] RM4001-8000
   [ ] RM8001and above

Part II:

Please rate your perception on the following statements by circling the numbers.

Strongly Disagree	Disagree	Neutral	Agree	Strongly Agree
1	2	3	4	5

A. Understanding about Corporate Social Responsibility (CSR)

No.	Items	SD	D	N	A	SA
1	I think I am familiar with the concept of Corporate Social Responsibility (CSR).	1	2	3	4	5

2. Which of the following issues are addressed by CSR. (Please tick all the right answers).

   Organizational Governance [ ]
   Human Rights [ ]
   Labour Practices [ ]
   Environment [ ]
   Fair Operating Practices [ ]
   Consumer Issues [ ]
   Community Involvement and Development [ ]

3. Are you aware of any companies operating in Malaysia that can be considered socially responsible?

   Yes [ ]　　　No [ ]

B. Consumer Awareness of Corporate Social Responsibility (CSR)

No.	Items	SD	D	N	A	SA
1	I care about environmental protection.	1	2	3	4	5
2	I pay attention to social issues.	1	2	3	4	5
3	I buy quality and/or inexpensive products, regardless of whether the provider is socially responsible or not.	1	2	3	4	5
4	I think that corporations play responsible roles in society.	1	2	3	4	5

D. Consumer's Trust in CSR

No.	Items	SD	D	N	A	SA
1	I think a company's socially responsible actions sincerely contribute to Malaysia.	1	2	3	4	5
2	I think companies take a lot of effort to be socially responsible.	1	2	3	4	5
3	I think a company's socially responsible practises can make a substantial contribution to Malaysia.	1	2	3	4	5
4	I view companies that practise CSR in a more positive manner.	1	2	3	4	5

F. Willingness to Pay Premium Price for CSR Products

CSR products are products for which a price premium is required to be charged on the consumers due to the social characteristic of that product. Such as organic food, free trade coffee.

No.	Items	SD	D	N	A	SA
1	I am willing to buy CSR product even though choices are limited.	1	2	3	4	5
2	I am willing to buy CSR products because the benefits outweigh the cost.	1	2	3	4	5
3	Buying CSR product is the right thing to do even if they cost more.	1	2	3	4	5
4	I don't mind spending more time sourcing for CSR product.	1	2	3	4	5
5	I would still buy CSR product even though conventional alternatives are on sale.	1	2	3	4	5

G. Purchase Intention

No.	Items	SD	D	N	A	SA
1	I will purchase a product because the company pays attention to charity activities.	1	2	3	4	5
2	I would pay more to buy products from a socially responsible corporation.	1	2	3	4	5

| 3 | If the price and quality of two products are the same, I would buy from the firm with a socially responsible reputation. | 1 | 2 | 3 | 4 | 5 |
| 4 | I will return to purchase a product again if the company has strong society responsibility. | 1 | 2 | 3 | 4 | 5 |

www.ingramcontent.com/pod-product-compliance
Lightning Source LLC
Chambersburg PA
CBHW030920180526
45163CB00002B/415